ENERGY,
ECONOMIC GROWTH,
AND EQUITY IN
THE UNITED STATES

ENERGY, ECONOMIC GROWTH, AND EQUITY IN THE UNITED STATES

Narasimhan P. Kannan

PRAEGER PUBLISHERS
Praeger Special Studies

New York • London • Sydney • Toronto

065945

Library of Congress Cataloging in Publication Data

Kannan, Narasimhan P
  Energy, economic growth, and equity in the United
States.

  Includes bibliographical references and index.
  1. Energy policy--United States--Mathematical
models. 2. United States--Economic poligy--1971-
--Mathematical models. I. Title.
HD9502.U52K35   333.7   78-31204
ISBN 0-03-046616-4

HD
9502
· U52
K35
1979

PRAEGER PUBLISHERS
PRAEGER SPECIAL STUDIES
383 Madison Avenue, New York, N.Y. 10017, U.S.A.

Published in the United States of America in 1979
by Praeger Publishers,
A Division of Holt, Rinehart and Winston, CBS, Inc.

9   038   987654321

© 1979 by Praeger Publishers

Printed in the United States of America

For My Parents
Pattu and Babu

PREFACE

Four decades ago the late John Maynard Keynes, with his characteristic sense of optimism, envisioned the seventies as an era when "science and compound interest" would have solved the economic problem of basic human needs. Until as recently as fifteen years ago, one would have admired Keynes for his foresight. Since then however, the turn of events has proved him wrong.

Decades of economic growth in the United States, although improving the lot of many, have failed to solve the problem of poverty. Islands of acute poverty persist amidst affluence even today, invalidating the conventional wisdom that "a growing economy lifts everyone." For better or for worse, economic growth has been mainly dependent upon to solve the problem of poverty, and the insidious energy crisis that confronts us today threatens this economic growth, and hence, the dream of an equitable society. For this reason it is important to consider all the potential consequences of energy policies that are designed to help achieve energy self-sufficiency. For instance, a policy may potentially solve the energy problem, but only at the expense of economic growth, which may cause the worst-off economic group today to be much worse off in the future. Thus, there may be implicit trade-offs between energy independence and economic growth (and hence, equity).

In this study alternate energy policies are identified and compared for their relative degrees of potential trade-offs. The evaluation of the policies is carried out with the aid of two computer simulation models, ECONOMY1 and FOSSIL1, which are designed to capture the interactions between the energy sector and the rest of the economy of the United States.

Various analyses of the energy/economy interactions found in the literature have been based on the neoclassical static equilibrium model, which is far from adequate to represent the essentially dynamic nature of the modern U.S. economy. Furthermore, the neoclassical model is based on unrealistic assumptions of perfect competition and profit and utility maximization. This study proposes an alternate set of hypotheses that emphasize the dynamics of social conflict over the distributive shares in the economy. The ECONOMY1 model is based on these hypotheses. It is hoped that this work will stimulate constructive debates among model builders and help in arriving at new and innovative approaches to analyzing the complex interactions between the energy sector and the rest of the economy.

ACKNOWLEDGMENTS

This research was carried out while I was a research assistant at the Thayer School of Engineering, Dartmouth College, from 1975 to 1977, as a part of the work performed under ERDA (Energy Research and Development Administration [now the Department of Energy]) Contract No. E(49-18)-2230. The excellent library and computer facilities at Dartmouth were of great help in this project.

This book would not have been possible but for the long hours of assistance, critique, and support from Leslie Madden, of Georgetown University Law Center. I am grateful for many of her important suggestions.

I also would like to express my appreciation to Professors Dennis Meadows, Roger Naill, and Dana Meadows, all of Dartmouth System Dynamics Group, and Dean Carl Long of the Thayer School, for giving me the opportunity to do this work, and for their useful comments. I am particularly indebted to Professors Gordon MacDonald of the Dartmouth Environmental Studies Program, and Richard Bower and George Oldfield of the Amos Tuck School for their encouragement and advice.

During the course of this work, I have received many valuable suggestions from Samir Salama, Roger Brown, George Backus, William Behrens, Howard Morland, and Desikan Bharathan, most of them my colleagues at the Thayer School. I gained many insights from Mel Donavan of Lyme, New Hampshire, whose persistent late-night debates contributed much to the treatment of the equity issue.

I am also grateful for the considerable research assistance provided by Phyllis Jaynes, librarian of the Feldberg Library at Dartmouth.

Without the help and encouragement of Wilbert Mueller, Harry Litwin, Owen McEwen, Jake Carey, Lyle Yost, and Edwin Law, all prominent businessmen from the State of Kansas, this work could not have been completed. I am most grateful for their timely help, both financial and intellectual.

Finally, I would like to thank Jane Andrele for her excellent artwork.

CONTENTS

LIST OF TABLES

LIST OF FIGURES

ENERGY, ECONOMIC GROWTH, AND EQUITY IN THE UNITED STATES

1

INTRODUCTION

The United States is presently entering a period of transition from dependency on cheap oil and natural gas for its energy needs[1] to reliance on more expensive alternatives such as coal, and nuclear, solar, and geothermal resources. Currently the nation is dependent on oil imports to make up the imbalance between domestic energy demand and supply. In 1977, for example, roughly 22 percent of the total energy consumed in the United States came from imports.[2] Such a dependence on imports is considered undesirable, since it makes the nation vulnerable to potential oil embargos by exporting countries. Furthermore, a recent study suggests that there may be global oil shortages in the coming decade, which may restrict or limit the amount of oil the United States can import.[3] In order to insulate the nation from potential oil embargos and world oil shortages during the energy transition period, policy makers in government are currently involved in the design of a national energy plan, which was proposed by President Carter in April 1977.† The primary goal of this plan is to create incentives that can lead to the correction of the domestic energy imbalance through conservation and increased domestic energy production.

A striking feature of the energy problem is the prospect of rising energy costs during the coming decades. It is suggested that the average price paid for energy may rise by a factor of three or

---

†Recently the Congress passed a watered-down version of this bill after considerable debates on appropriate policies for stimulating domestic production. These debates are bound to intensify in the coming years as we become increasingly dependent on foreign oil.

1

more from its present level, by the year 2000.[5] The rising energy cost is a reflection of the declining productivity of capital in the energy sector. This decline is caused partly by depletion of oil and gas, partly by environmental and safety requirements in the production and use of coal and nuclear resources, and partly by expensive new technologies such as solar- and coal-conversion. The falling productivity in the energy sector could adversely affect economic growth by contributing to a decline in overall national productivity. However, this effect could be countered by substitution for energy of capital, labor, and other inputs. Thus, to what degree substitution may offset the effects of falling productivity becomes an important question.

A recent analysis suggests that energy consumption is closely related to gross national product and that a decline in energy consumption will lead to a decline in output.[6] This analysis is based on the historical relationship between percent change in annual energy consumption and percent change in real gross national product (shown in Figure 1.1). The implication here is that energy is a nonsubstitutable commodity. In the short run it is likely that economic growth is closely related to energy consumption. In the long run, however, substitution possibilities such as insulation of structures and use of smaller automobiles could change the relationship between energy use and economic growth. Thus, in addition to the degree of substitutability, the time delays involved in substitution also affect future economic growth.

The National Energy Plan, proposed by the current administration, calls for continued economic growth.[7] Whether economic growth can be sustained while solving the energy problem is a question of paramount importance to policy makers. Any attempt to address this issue requires a detailed study of the interactions between the energy sector and the rest of the economy.

The area of energy/economy interactions is one of enormous complexity, due to the fundamental role of energy in everyday activities. The methods of analysis available for studying these interactions leave a great deal to be desired.[8] However, there is great interest in improving these techniques; for example, recently a whole conference was devoted to the examination of currently available methods of analysis of energy/economy interactions.[9]

One possible approach to analyzing energy/economy interactions is developed in this study, with the object of assessing the impact on the economy due to alternate possible contingencies of energy availability and energy prices in the future. With the aid of two computer simulation models, FOSSIL1 and ECONOMY1, the effects of alternate energy policy options on the long-term economic

FIGURE 1.1

The Historical Relationship between Energy and Economic Growth

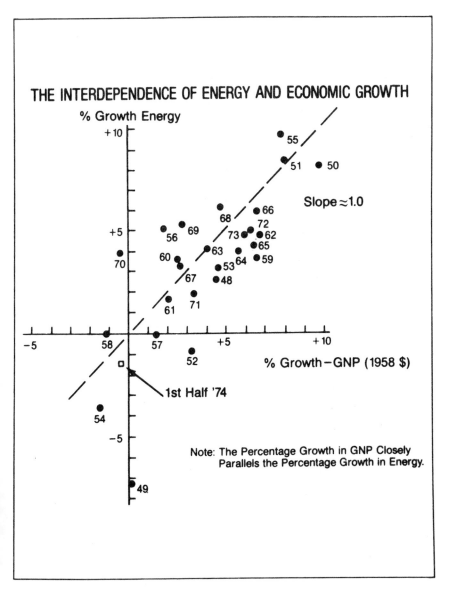

Source: Ford Foundation, A Time to Choose: America's Energy Future (Cambridge, Mass.: Ballinger, 1974), p. 368. Reprinted with permission.

growth are assessed. The study does not address short-term issues such as inflation, unemployment, and interest rate fluctuations.

In addition to economic growth, a second important issue is the effect of rising energy prices on low-income groups in the country.[10] The concern over this issue is reflected in one of the principles that guided the formulation of the National Energy Plan, which states that ". . . The United States must solve its energy problems in a manner that is equitable to all regions, sectors, and income groups. . . . In particular, the elderly, the poor, and those on fixed incomes should be protected from disproportionately adverse effects on their income."[11] This principle implies that protection of the poor must come through transfer payments. In a slow growth economy, for example, it may become increasingly difficult to subsidize the poor without causing a reduction in the standard of living of the rest. The current popular sentiment against high taxes may gain momentum in the future and may make the prospect of increasing transfer payment to the poor politically infeasible.[†] Therefore it becomes necessary for policy makers to understand the implications for the distribution of income of alternate energy policies.

In this study, using aggregate economic variables such as the gross national product, and the shares of national income going to capital, labor, and the energy sectors of the domestic economy, certain cautious inferences have been made that bear on the equity issue. In addition, important directions for future research have been identified.

The most dominant factor with a potential for influencing the course of the U.S. economy is depletion of conventional energy sources—oil and gas. It has been suggested that within the next four decades oil and gas reserves around the world may have become so depleted that the fuels are available only for high-priced uses.[12] For this reason the time horizon of the present study was chosen to extend from 1950 to 2020. The first 26 years are used for testing the model's ability to replicate historical behavior modes of various economic variables. The rest of the time horizon is used to test the implications of alternate energy policies.

This book is organized into five chapters. In the second chapter the neoclassical approach to analyzing the energy/economy interactions is described and some of its shortcomings are identified. In the third chapter a set of new hypotheses is developed. These

------

[†]One example of revolt against high taxes is the recent referendum in the state of California on Proposition 13 which is designed to cut property taxes significantly.

hypotheses relate to the important dynamic mechanisms through which the energy sector and the rest of the economy interact. These hypotheses are incorporated within the structure of a formal model, presented in the fourth chapter. In Chapter 5 the model is used to evaluate the relative merits of alternate energy policy options on growth and distribution of income. Finally, a set of conclusions are drawn from the results of policy analyses.

NOTES

1. For a detailed description of the energy transition problem, see Ford Foundation, A Time to Choose: America's Energy Future (Cambridge, Mass.: Ballinger, 1974); and Roger F. Naill, Managing the Energy Transition (Cambridge, Mass.: Ballinger, 1977), Ch. 1.

2. Based on the estimates given in the National Energy Plan, Executive Office of the President (Washington, D.C.: U.S. Government Printing Office, 1977), p. 14.

3. World oil shortages are forecast in Carrol Wilson, Energy—Global Prospects, 1985-2000, Report of the Workshop on Alternative Energy Strategies (New York: McGraw-Hill, 1977). Estimates made by the U.S. Central Intelligence Agency, on which the National Energy Plan is based, support Wilson's study.

4. For details of the plan, see National Energy Plan.

5. See, for example, Report of the Nuclear Energy Policy Study Group, Nuclear Power Issues and Choices (Cambridge, Mass.: Ballinger, 1977), p. 51; and Table 9 in Dale W. Jorgenson and Edward A. Hudson, "U.S. Energy Policy and Economic Growth, 1975-2000," Bell Journal of Economics and Management Science 5 (Autumn 1974): 461-514.

6. This analysis was presented by D. C. Burnham in his critique of the Ford Foundation study, A Time to Choose, p. 368.

7. National Energy Plan, p. 26.

8. Four of the recent analyses of energy/economy interactions are evaluated in Chapter 2 of this book: Dale W. Jorgenson and Edward A. Hudson, "U.S. Energy Policy and Economic Growth, 1975-2000"; David J. Behling, Jr., Robert Dullien, and Edward A. Hudson, The Relationship of Energy Growth Under Alternative Energy Policies (Upton, N.Y.: Brookhaven National Laboratory), BNL-50500, March 1976; William W. Hogan and Alan S. Manne, "Energy-Economy Interactions: The Fable of the Elephant and the Rabbit?" Energy Modeling Forum Working Paper, Stanford University, Stanford, California, November 1976; and Edward L. Allen et al., U.S. Energy and Economic Growth, Institute for Energy Analysis, Oak Ridge Associated Universities, Oak Ridge, Tennessee, September 1976.

9. See Proceedings of the Workshop on Modeling the Inter-relationships Between the Energy Sector and General Economy, EPRI SR-45, Electric Power Research Institute, Palo Alto, California, July 1976.

10. Marc Roberts, "Economic Consequences of Energy Costs," in Energy and Man, ed. M. Granger Morgan (New York: IEEE Press, 1975), pp. 466-79. Also see A Time To Choose, Ch. 5, for a treatment of the equity problem.

11. National Energy Plan, p. 27.

12. Wilson, Energy—Global Prospects, 1985-2000, pp. 8-9.

2

THE NEOCLASSICAL APPROACH

Most of the recent analyses of the energy/economy interactions are based on the neoclassical model of production.[1] In this chapter the basic assumptions of the neoclassical model are described and some of the recent studies based on it reviewed. It will be established that though the static neoclassical approach casts considerable light on the energy/economy interactions that may take place in a hypothetical economy, it is far from adequate to deal with the essentially dynamic character of adjustment processes in the real world of the U.S. economy.

THE BASIC ASSUMPTIONS
OF THE NEOCLASSICAL MODEL

The neoclassical model[2] is based on the following assumptions:

A market economy, such as that of the United States, consists of rational firms that always strive to maximize their profits in delivering goods and services to consumers.

The firms employ a set of factors of production, capital, and labor, whose prices are determined solely by the free market forces of supply and demand.

The supply of factors of production is dependent on the market price of factors and the utility function of the owners of the factors. For example, members of the labor force allocate their time between work and leisure by maximizing their utility, given the price for their services. Similarly, capital owners allocate their resources between current and future consumption by maximizing their utility, given the price for the services of capital.

In short, these assumptions are generally referred to as perfect competition and profit maximization assumptions.

Equipped with these assumptions, analysts treat the problem of energy/economy interactions as follows. Energy is viewed as an input factor just as capital and labor are inputs to the production of goods and services. When energy becomes scarce, the market-determined price of energy will rise, and the firms will respond to this rise by substituting capital, labor, and other resources which are relatively less expensive than energy. In general, the firms respond to a scarcity of one factor by optimizing the mix of factors used in production in such a manner that profits will be maximized. The ease with which such substitutions can be achieved by firms is measured by a parameter known as the elasticity of substitution. This parameter is critical in assessing the impact of energy scarcity on the rest of the economy.

The following example illustrates the significance of the elasticity parameter. Assume that E denotes the energy input to the production of goods and services and R denotes all other factors lumped together. Now, the elasticity of substitution, denoted by S, measures the degree of substitutability between E and R when their relative price changes. A 1 percent increase in energy price relative to the price of R would lead to an S percent increase in the ratio of R to E. This ratio determines the mix of R and E that will be used for factor input by the firms. The concept of elasticity of substitution is useful in analyzing the response of firms in the nonenergy sector of the economy to a rise in energy price. The elasticity parameter, however, does not say anything about the time rate at which substitution proceeds, but only about the equilibrium mix of factors of production. In fact, most neoclassical models implicitly assume instantaneous substitution processes. This is clearly a drawback when one is interested in the time rate of the factor mix adjustment process.

The elasticity of substitution is a technical coefficient, meaning that it is determined by the state of the technology of production. This coefficient ranges from zero to positive infinity. For processes where the elasticity is close to zero it is extremely difficult to substitute other inputs for energy. Thus, if energy becomes scarce, the economy suffers in terms of reduced output. On the other hand, if the elasticity of substitution is a high positive number, then capital and/or labor can be substituted for energy relatively easily, and the effect of energy scarcity on output will be minimal.

Generally, a typical neoclassical analysis proceeds by estimating the elasticity-of-substitution parameter from historical time-series data on factor prices and factor mixes used in the production process. In estimating this parameter, it is assumed that the domestic economy functions in compliance with the assumptions of perfect competition and profit maximization. An important reason for this unrealistic assumption is mathematical convenience.

The neoclassical model lends itself to an extremely simple and elegant mathematical representation of the aggregate production system.† The most important component of the mathematical model of the neoclassical production system is known as the aggregate production function. The production function is a technical relationship between the factor inputs and the maximum output that can be achieved using the known technology. The production function is generally chosen to reflect the basic properties of the production technology involved in the process under analysis. For example, the production function should reflect the fact that if all inputs are reduced to zero the output must likewise be zero. Furthermore, if any one factor input is increased indefinitely, the output will rise less than proportionately and thus satisfy the law of diminishing returns. The production function also contains information in analytical form about the elasticity of substitution between factors. Thus, in a neoclassical framework, if one knows the form of the production function and the prices of factor inputs and the output, then the optimal factor mix can be found by maximizing profits (revenues minus costs) subject to the constraint of the production function.

At this point it may be useful to consider, briefly, three of the recent studies that attempt to analyze the energy/economy interactions and predict the impact of rising energy costs on economic growth. The three studies are the Energy Modeling Forum (EMF) study being conducted at Stanford University, the Institute for Energy Analysis (IEA) study, and the Hudson-Jorgenson study.[3] Brief technical descriptions of these analyses are provided for the interested reader in Appendix A. In what follows a brief verbal treatment is presented.

THE ENERGY MODELING FORUM STUDY

The EMF analysis uses a production function model based on the neoclassical assumptions. The analysis focusses on the criticality of the elasticity-of-substitution parameter (between energy and other inputs to production) and suggests that the future level of the gross national product is dependent on the value of this parameter.

---

†A brief mathematical development of the neoclassical production model is given in Appendix A.

In this analysis the authors assume a base case consisting of a set of equilibrium values of energy consumption, price of energy, and gross national product at a point in the future, and compute the change in the assumed gross national product for a given change in energy consumption for various values of the elasticity of substitution. (These results are summarized in Table A.1.) This method of analysis is known as the comparative statics approach. Using this method, the authors demonstrate that the elasticity-of-substitution parameter is highly sensitive in determining the future course of the economy and that accurate measurement of this parameter is a matter of great importance.

Despite the limited scope of the EMF study, the authors conclude that the energy sector may not adversely affect future economic growth. They reach this conclusion by suggesting that the elasticity of substitution between energy and other input factors is fairly high. The study does not report any empirical verification of the claim of the authors.

In summary, the EMF study uses a static equilibrium analysis of the energy/economy interaction and does not address the issues of time lags involved in the factor substitution process.

THE INSTITUTE FOR ENERGY ANALYSIS STUDY

The IEA study addresses the issue of potential decline in national factor productivity due to a decline in the productivity in the energy sector. The authors present a simple scheme through which the magnitude of decline in aggregate productivity can be computed, given a certain decline in energy sector productivity.

In Figure 2.1 a causal representation of the IEA model is shown. As energy costs rise due to a decline in energy capital productivity, the total factor productivity declines and causes the output (gross national product) to fall. As output declines, the net aggregate investment declines for a given savings rate, and after a certain time lag, the growth rate of capital stock is adversely affected. In the model it is assumed that the labor force, productivity, energy costs, savings rate, and depreciation rate are exogenous variables. In addition, the energy sector's influence on aggregate productivity is assumed to be a function of the energy sector's factor share of national product. The study takes the historical factor share of the energy sector to be 1.5 percent of the gross national product.[4] Using this estimate, the authors of the IEA study suggest that even if energy costs triple over the next three decades, the impact on economic growth will be minimal, since the energy sector's share of output will still only be 4.5 percent of total output.

FIGURE 2.1

A Causal Representation of the Institute for Energy Analysis Model

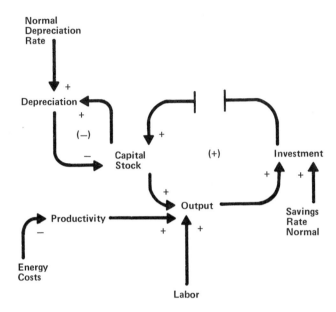

Note: The causal representation shown above and others in this book provide useful illustrations of the structure of the model in question. In this diagram, each link indicates the influence of one variable on the other. The positive or negative sign indicates the polarity of influence, holding all other factors constant. A break in the link indicates a time lag. For example, investment influences the capital stock positively after a time delay.

Source: Constructed by the author.

The IEA study's conclusion is highly sensitive to the value share assumption and it is not clear from the study how the historical value of 1.5 percent was derived. Furthermore, the study does not consider the substitution processes by which energy demand could be reduced.

THE HUDSON-JORGENSON STUDY

The Hudson-Jorgenson study employs an extremely sophisticated mathematical model to analyze the energy/economy interactions.

FIGURE 2.2

A Schematic Representation of the
Hudson–Jorgenson Model Interactions

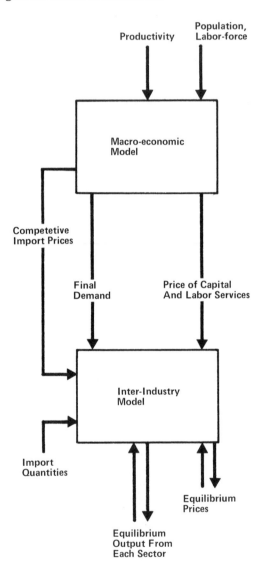

Note: No feedback from the interindustry model to the macro
model exists.

Source: Constructed by the author.

12

The model is poorly documented and hence difficult to comprehend by someone not familiar with the implicit assumptions. Despite its complexity, it is based on the simple neoclassical assumptions of perfect competition and profit maximization. The model is used by the authors to generate a set of equilibrium solutions of quantities and prices of output from the following nine sectors of the U.S. economy: agriculture, non-fuel mining, and construction; manufacturing, excluding petroleum refining; transportation; communications, trade, and services; coal mining; crude petroleum and natural gas; electric utilities; gas utilities; and petroleum refining.

These nine sectors are set in an input/output framework and the coefficients of the input/output matrix are determined endogenously as a function of factor prices and the price of imported oil.[5] The model requires four input factors: capital, labor, energy, and other materials.

The nine-sector interindustry model interacts with another, macroeconomic model of the U.S. economy, which is a two-sector, neoclassical model with capital goods and consumption goods as the two sectors.[6] This model is used to generate the prices of capital and labor services endogenously, and these prices are used in the interindustry model as inputs. In Figure 2.2 a schematic diagram of the Hudson-Jorgenson model is shown.

The Hudson-Jorgenson model suffers from two major shortcomings. One is that there is no feedback from the interindustry model to the macroeconomic growth model. Thus, the model could not be consistently used to assess the impact on economic growth of alternate energy availability or price scenarios. The second attribute is that in the interindustry model the substitutions among factors are assumed to occur with no time lags. The delays involved in substituting capital, labor, or materials for energy may be significant in determining the physical rate at which substitution can occur. For example, a recent study suggests that "While much can be done in a short time to tighten energy use in existing plants, buildings and transportation systems, it will take years, even decades, to fully replace old stock with more efficient new equipment."[7] Thus, these two drawbacks bias the model forecasts in an optimistic direction.

The Hudson-Jorgenson model is designed to answer one question specifically: What is the effect of alternate energy tax (conservation) policies on the equilibrium outputs and prices in the nine-sector model economy? The authors reach a set of highly optimistic conclusions regarding the potential for substitution of other factors for energy in the future. Their conclusions are highly questionable, considering the fact that parameter estimates used in the model are primarily based on pre-embargo time-series data. In other words, an implicit assumption in the Hudson-Jorgenson model is that, in the future, other factors can be substituted for energy with the same ease with which energy was substituted for other factors during the past three decades. During the pre-embargo years energy prices were highly stable compared to the prices of other inputs. Thus, history is hardly representative of how the U.S. economy would adjust in a resource-scarce environment. It is not clear whether historical data from a nonrepresentative period are useful in determining the degree and rate of factor substitution in the future. Thus, it is not surprising that the Hudson-Jorgenson study has led to optimistic conclusions, since the assumptions are unduly optimistic.

SUMMARY

In summary, it seems reasonable to generalize that the static, neoclassical equilibrium analysis of energy/economy interactions is most likely to lead to optimistic conclusions regarding the effect of high energy prices on economic growth. The optimistic results stem principally from the assumptions of perfect competition and instantaneous factor substitution processes. The neoclassical model calls for an emphasis on the equilibrium state of the economy rather than the dynamic behavior modes or the adjustment paths. Time lags can be easily introduced in the neoclassical model, but the analysis will become complex if the profit maximization and perfect competition assumptions are relaxed. To this extent, the neoclassical analysis does not provide the flexibility needed to test alternate assumptions of imperfect competition and nonmaximizing behavior of economic entities. Thus, the neoclassical approach leads to analysis of energy/economy interactions based on a unique view of reality. There is a need to analyze these interactions under an alternate set of assumptions to test the sensitivity of projections of economic variables into the future.

A strong case could be made for testing alternate assumptions regarding nonmaximizing behavior and delays in substitution processes. For instance, one of the major conclusions that emerged from a recent conference on modeling the energy/economy interactions states: "Whatever approaches are chosen for modeling the interrelationships between the energy sector and the rest of the economy, the emerging models must be able to address the major institutional constraints that govern these interrelationships. They must be able to deal with the impacts of resource exhaustion, the implications of non-optimizing behavior, and the dynamics of the adjustment process."[8] The dynamics of the adjustment process in this statement point to what is commonly known as the disequilibrium effect. A disequilibrium model focusses on the path of the market-clearing process rather than on the end result of the equilibrium state. Furthermore the nonoptimizing behavior, alluded to in the above quote, suggests that the assumption of nonmaximization of profits by firms needs to be tested for its impact on the energy/ economy interactions. In this study the assumptions regarding nonmaximizing behavior and the dynamics of adjustment processes are tested for their implications on future U.S. economic growth.

THE CHOICE OF A METHOD

In this study the system dynamics method was chosen to model the energy/economy interactions.[9] The system dynamics paradigm places emphasis on the disequilibrium paths, rather than the equilibrium points; on the complex nature of information-feedback loops and system nonlinearities, rather than on elegant closed-form mathematical solutions; on the system structure rather than on the empirical values of parameters. These attributes make this method suitable for addressing the energy/economy interactions in a realistic manner. The system dynamics method suggests that every socioeconomic system behaves according to the dictates of a latent causal structure that changes very slowly over time. If one can systematically synthesize the underlying structure from the existing descriptive knowledge of the system components, then, through deductive reasoning, meaningful statements can be made regarding the future state of the system, and hence, about its future behavior. Thus, any statement about the future is necessarily a conditional one, and therefore it is important that the conditions or assumptions on which a set of projections are based be as realistic as possible. The method of system dynamics allows one to test the implications of a wide variety of behavioral hypotheses. More important, a model based on the system dynamics method affords the flexibility needed to test for system behavior outside the historical range. For example, there is no absolute empirical basis from which to study the effect of oil and gas depletion on the future course of the U.S. economy, since there is no information on how a modern industrial society would respond to such externalities.[†] This dilemma is clearly

---

†For example, the neoclassical economic science, modeled after the physical science counterparts, rejects the notion of "a priori." Therefore, any statement regarding the behavior of the economy is required by economic science to have a strong empirical basis. In contrast, the system dynamics paradigm allows a priori concep-

illustrated by the EMF study, discussed earlier, on the matter of elasticity of substitution. On this issue, Jay Forrester, the originator of the system dynamics method, suggests, "One important use for a model is to explore system behavior outside the normal and historical ranges of operation. These ranges will be outside the region of any data that could have been collected in the past. We are dependent on our insight into the separate parts of the system to establish how they would respond to new circumstances."[10]

In a data-rich environment for developing formal mathematical representations of reality, there is no excuse for not using the empirical body of knowledge. Unfortunately, the realities of pollution and resource depletion are not well understood and data are not readily available, and yet they need immediately attention on the part of government. The policy makers cannot afford to wait for the facts to accumulate in order to then have a strong empirical basis for decision making. Policies regarding energy use in the United States must be implemented today to achieve self-sufficiency goals by the year 2010. This calls for models of the economy to be developed today, to aid the policy makers who are involved in shaping the uncertain future. In this regard, the system dynamics method is highly suited for analyzing the energy/economy interactions and designing policies which, while helping achieve energy independence, will not adversely affect economic growth in the future.

In the following chapter, a set of hypotheses regarding the structure of the U.S. economy is presented. These hypotheses are incorporated into a formal representation of the aggregate U.S. economy, which is described in Chapter 4.

NOTES

1. For an elementary treatment of the neoclassical theory, see R. G. D. Allen, Macro-Economic Theory—A Mathematical Treatment (New York: Macmillan, 1968). For a more general treatment, see Kazuo Sato, Production Functions and Aggregation (Amsterdam: North-Holland Publishing Co., 1975); L. Johansen, Production Functions (Amsterdam: North-Holland Publishing Co., 1972);

---

tualization of a structure of the system under scrutiny. Without such a structure, the fragmentary empirical information available to the senses would be devoid of meaning. Thus, the system dynamics method has a basis in Kantian rationalism as opposed to the logical positivistic basis of neoclassical economics.[11]

and Edwin Burmeister and Rodney A. Dobell, Mathematical Theories of Economic Growth (New York: Macmillan, 1970). For an extensive survey of production and cost functions, see A. A. Walters, "Production and Cost Functions," Econometrica 31 (April 1963): 1-66. Also see Paul A. Samuelson, Foundations of Economic Analysis (Cambridge, Mass.: Harvard University Press, 1947), Chs. 2 and 4, for a lucid presentation of the neoclassical equilibrium analysis of production.

2. See Allen, Macro-Economic Theory, pp. 44-55, for a brief description of the basic neoclassical model of production and distribution.

3. The Energy Modeling Forum at Stanford University is presently involved in a comparative study of various models of energy/economy interactions. The forum circulated a paper entitled "Energy-Economy Interactions: The Fable of the Elephant and the Rabbit?," authored by William W. Hogan and Allan S. Manne in November 1976. This paper, which is unpublished, is reviewed in this chapter. The other studies reviewed in this chapter are Edward L. Allen et al., U.S. Energy and Economic Growth (Oak Ridge, Tenn.: The Institute for Energy Analysis, September 1976); and Dale W. Jorgenson and Edward A. Hudson, "U.S. Energy Policy and Economic Growth, 1975-2000," Bell Journal of Economics and Management Science 5 (Autumn 1974): 461-514.

4. For instance, the IEA study's assumption is given on p. 130 of Allen et al., U.S. Energy and Economic Growth, and this value of 1.5 percent is rather low compared to the 5 percent estimates of other studies. See Mitre Corporation, Nuclear Power Issues and Choices (Cambridge, Mass.: Ballinger, 1977), p. 49; and the EMF paper, "Energy-Economy Interactions," p. 3.

5. The input/output framework is developed in detail in Wassily W. Leontief, The Structure of the American Economy 1919-1939 (New York: Oxford University Press, 1951); and in Wassily W. Leontief, Studies in the Structure of the American Economy (New York: Oxford University Press, 1953).

6. The two-sector neoclassical growth model is presented in Burmeister and Dobell, Mathematical Theories of Economic Growth.

7. Ford Foundation, A Time to Choose (Cambridge, Mass.: Ballinger, 1974), p. 77.

8. Proceedings of the Workshop on Modeling the Interrelationships Between the Energy Sector and General Economy, EPRI SR-45, Electric Power Research Institute, Palo Alto, California, July 1976, p. VII-6.

9. The basic concepts of system dynamics are presented in Jay W. Forrester, Industrial Dynamics (Cambridge, Mass.: M.I.T. Press, 1961).

10. Forrester, Industrial Dynamics, p. 59.

11. For a description of the methods of economics see Milton Friedman, "The Methodology of Positive Economics," in Essays in Positive Economics (Chicago, Ill.: University of Chicago Press, 1953). An excellent critique of the positive economics is presented by Martin Hollis and Edward Nell, Rational Economic Man, A Philosophical Critique of Neo-Classical Economics (New York: Cambridge University Press, 1975).

3

AN ALTERNATIVE APPROACH—
THEORETICAL DESCRIPTIONS

INTRODUCTION

In the last chapter the basic neoclassical model of production and three recent studies based on this model were reviewed. These models focussed on an ideal, hypothetical economy and attempted to make predictions about the future state of the real system. In this chapter, an alternate approach to modeling energy/economy interactions is presented and it emphasizes realism rather than idealism in developing a model of the U.S. economic system with the hope that it will be more useful to policy makers than models based on the neoclassical theory.

Since the structure of a model is derived from a causal theory regarding the interaction of the system elements, it is imperative that the theory, which is but one view of the real system, be described in detail to aid in its scrutiny by model builders with alternate paradigms. Therefore, a detailed verbal statement of a set of postulates concerning the structure of the U.S. economy is provided in this chapter. The following chapter will give a more formal representation of the macroeconomic model, which is based on the theories developed in this section.

In order to study energy/economy interactions it is necessary to have a clear understanding of the interactions among major system elements in the aggregate economy—for example, the causal factors affecting growth in output. To facilitate this understanding, three major hypotheses will be stated, described, and interpreted. These hypotheses relate to factor substitution process, the role of technology in increasing factor productivity, and the savings and investment process which aids in the accumulation of capital. These three factors largely govern the long-term behavior of the economic system.

It must be noted that the hypotheses presented here are not statements of facts. They are merely a set of descriptive statements of one possible perception of reality. The following statement by James Duesenberry, a caveat about the statement of his savings and investment hypothesis, applies here equally well.

> What we have done is to present a hypothesis about consumer behavior and work out some of its implications. In the nature of the case we have had to over-simplify. Much of the richness and variety of real life must be lost in developing a hypothesis which can be stated formally. Moreover, we have not proved our hypothesis. Indeed we cannot. All we can do is set up a theory which seems plausible in the light of general observation and of psychological conditions. Having done that we can see whether the implications for the hypothesis are consistent with available data. If they are, we can tentatively accept the hypothesis. But we have to recognize that new data may break it down at any time.[1]

THE NATURE OF MARKETS

Conventional economic theory views the economy as a set of markets where producers, motivated by potential opportunities for profits, and consumers, guided by a set of preferences, meet to exchange goods and services. At the end of such an exchange process, all markets—labor, capital, and product—clear, giving rise to a set of equilibrium prices with no surpluses or deficits of goods and service production capacities. Furthermore, no single participant in the market exchange process has power to influence either the prices or the quantities exchanged. Such is the nature of the competitive equilibrium process. As seen in the previous chapter, most models of long-term economic growth assume the existence of perfect competition and profit and utility maximization. Unfortunately, this view is neither realistic nor perfectly useful in studying modern industrial economies.[†] It is unrealistic to assume that markets will

---

[†] Most economists would readily admit that the free-market model does not accurately represent the U.S. economy. Despite its inapplicability, the free-market model is used extensively in almost all the formal analyses presented in scholarly journals. Policy

ever reach an equilibrium state. If, for example, the economy could be frozen at some instant, and if scientific observations could be made on the state of the participants, then one would be bound to observe various levels of fears, expectations, and intentions among the participants. It is indeed a rare situation where utility of participants is maximized. Fears regarding layoffs, regulations, and public opinion; expectations of inflation; and intentions of lobbying through the local congressman for work stoppage and for automation—all these and other similar factors characterize the state of the participants at any instant.

Rejecting the notion of perfect competition and profit and utility maximization as unrealistic is, however, easier than providing an alternate specification of the goal structure of socioeconomic institutions. Among several possible alternatives to the neoclassical model one recent suggestion seems to provide a realistic and useful description of the goal structure of the participants in the domestic economy. In his recent criticism of the standard economic theory, Nicholas Georgescu-Roegen states:

> Causal observation of what happens in the sphere of economic organizations, or between these organizations and individuals, suffices to reveal phenomena that do not consist of tâtonnement with given means towards given ends according to given rules. They show beyond any doubt that in all societies the typical individual continually pursues also an end ignored by the standard framework: the increase of what he can claim as his income according to his current position and distributive norms. It is the pursuit of this end that makes the individual a true agent of the economic process.[2]

In order to use the above suggestion as a basis for developing a model of the aggregate economy, it is useful to consider the diverse groups in the economy which are in a state of continuous conflict. For example, there are conflicts between capitalists who would like higher profits and laborers who want higher wages. Similarly, consumers want lower prices and producers higher profits. In essence, all these

---

recommendations coming out of these analyses eventually find their way among decision makers in the government. This should be a matter of serious concern, since policy recommendations based on spurious models could affect the lives of millions in an adverse manner.

groups are fighting to alter the distributive relations in their own favor.

Furthermore, a modern industrial economy consists of markets for factors of production and products, with the government as the chief consumer, arbiter, savior, intruder, regulator, and sometimes allocater. In resolving conflicts, the government has economic as well as legal power over the producers and consumers of most goods and services. For instance, the U.S. government commands power over the allocation of a third of the gross national product. Thus, the government cannot be viewed as an exogenous agent in the economic process. As Alfred Kahn suggests, "The 'government' is not a deus ex machina, 'exogenous' to the economic process. It is part of the process, and its decisions are themselves molded by the private economic interests it is supposed to control. Every government expenditure, tax, and money transfer has, not only a macroeconomic, but a microeconomic consequence as well, and, even more important, an impact on the economic welfare of some group of private parties."[3] Thus, there is not only a conflict among diverse groups over distributive shares of the product, but there is also a significant role played by the government to maintain a delicate balance between conflicting forces.

For the present purpose of analyzing the energy/economy interactions, it is useful to consider the distributional conflict among various economic entities. For example, the output from an economy can be imagined as a giant pie. Each of the groups in conflict wishes to have as much of this pie as possible, since a greater share implies a greater command over the allocation of the output. Some wish to allocate the output to wealth-producing assets and thus gain more command over the resource base in the future; others wish to consume the current output and thereby derive a feeling of well-being. Regardless of the intentions of a specific group, the basic desire common to all is to achieve and maintain power to command the allocation of output.[4] This may be the primary driving force in a modern economy, leading to inflation, growth, and the associated problems of resource depletion.[†]

[†] For instance, if it is assumed that firms pass on their costs to consumers, then any increase in wages would contribute to the wage-price spiral of inflation in the short run. Furthermore, it could be argued that growth in output results from pressures resulting from conflict over relative shares of income. For instance, in a growing economy, insidious gains made by one sector are tolerated, since no one will emerge as a loser in absolute terms. Without

To be more specific, the energy sector may influence the rest of the economy by causing a threat to the balance of power among the diverse entities in conflict. For example, increasingly expensive energy sources may tilt the balance of power in favor of the capital owners in the energy sector. Of course, the rest of the economy would respond to this prospect by attempting to retain their relative shares of the national output, and by conserving on the use of energy or through political means, would attempt to hold down energy prices. One of the primary means of conservation is substitution of other resources for energy. Thus, the process of substitution could be viewed as a consequence of the desire to maintain the distributive relationships.

A good indicator of the distribution of power over the allocation of output is the distribution of national income or the relative shares of output among conflicting groups. A hypothesis based on the relative shares is presented and described.

THE RELATIVE INCOME SHARE HYPOTHESIS

The disparate economic entities which constitute the national economy of a modern industrial state such as the United States, act, in the aggregate, as if to resist any reduction in their relative share of national output (income). †

To elaborate on the above statement of the relative income share hypothesis, it is illustrative to consider the goal-seeking behavior as represented for a single group in Figure 3.1. In this figure it is suggested that each of the groups in conflict tries to upgrade its relative status based on a discrepancy between a desired state and the actual state of distributive share of national income. Any disturbance—either internal or external to the economic system— that causes a change in the relative distributional share, leads to social, economic, and political actions or reactions that try to bring the system to its initial state. The adjustment process involves time lags, and the new state of the system after the response to the

---

growth, one sector cannot gain without reducing another's share, and the losers may become less than tolerant. This could lead to destructive social upheavals. Such a situation may be inevitable, due to the finite nature of many resources on which growth is based.

†Throughout this and the following chapters, relative income share between any two factors implies the ratio of income to the two factors.

FIGURE 3.1

A Causal Diagram Illustrating the Relative Income Share Theory

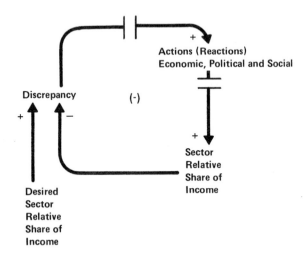

Source: Constructed by the author.

disturbance is determined by the most dominant of the resultant forces. Thus, the relative income share hypothesis could be viewed as a weak economic analogue to Newton's Third Law of Motion in mechanics, which states that action and reaction are equal and opposite.

In order to demonstrate the usefulness of the relative income share hypothesis, it is necessary to define the terms "economic entity," "disturbance," and "actions." The definitions are necessary for achieving a precise, formal representation of the hypothesis.

An economic entity, as used here, represents a homogeneous group of participants in the economy who share a common interest in increasing their share of the national output.† For example, a logical choice of a group that represents an economic entity would be the owners of factors of production. To be more precise, the economy can be considered to consist of N groups in conflict.

---

†For instance, the classification by Marx of economic agents into capitalists and laborers.

Further, let $(X_i)_t$ be the share of national output at time to to the i-th group, where $i = 1, 2, 3, \ldots, N$. Then by definition, if at some time t_1 any X_i approaches zero then all X_is will approach zero at some time greater than t_1. The above statement implies that each of the groups in conflict is absolutely essential to the functioning of the economy as a whole.

The second term that requires a precise definition is disturbance. Examples of disturbances are sudden rises in wages or rents, technological breakthroughs, monopoly pricing, depletion of finite resources, and natural calamity. Disturbances can arise from within the system or from without. Those from within are, for example, excessive gains made by labor in union negotiations on wages, monopoly rents charged by one sector of the economy, and a rise in tax rates on income and wealth. Those from without, over which the participants in the economic system have no control, are monopoly pricing by resource-exporting countries such as OPEC (Oil Producing and Exporting Countries), depletion of finite resources, and natural calamity. A disturbance can be defined as anything that causes a shift in the relative shares of the national income. The examples of internal disturbances indicated above are also simply the actions taken by individual groups in increasing their relative shares of the product.

Every disturbance, in turn, causes a sequence of actions and reactions by groups in conflict to maintain their relative positions. For instance, excessive wage gains are retaliated against by substitution of capital for labor and through investment in research and development for automating labor-intensive processes. This is an example of an economic reaction. Similarly, there are political reactions to disturbance of the relative shares. Examples of political actions or reactions are lobbying for higher tax credits, subsidies, protective tariffs, restricted membership in professions, minimum wages, and price regulation. Furthermore, there is an additional set of actions that could be classified as social actions. Propaganda through mass media and organized boycotts of products fall into this category.

It is important to note that the relative income share hypothesis does not suggest that each of the groups in conflict consciously measures and attempts to gain in relative status, but that its actions in the aggregate tend to be as if it attempts to maintain its relative status. Thus, the hypothesis stands as a useful and convenient abstraction, which could be viewed as a statement of a dynamic version of the well-known zero-sum game problem. [5]

A strong empirical basis that supports the relative income share hypothesis is the presence of inflation in modern economies. After an exhaustive analysis of the causes of inflation, Alfred Kahn concludes that price determination is "a dynamic process, as much political in the broadest sense as economic, by which various groups in the economy fight over their shares of national income."[6] Additional evidence that supports the relative share hypothesis is that there are frequently observed resistances to changes such as productivity-enhancing automation or computer control. C. C. von Weizsäcker, in analyzing certain barriers to growth in productivity, observes: "In the political process division of labor produces special interests of different sub-groups of a population. They will try to influence the political process to increase their share in the national product. They will resist change and progress, if it hurts their particular group. We can observe that the political process has a bias in favour of the demands of interest groups."[7]

The two examples cited above are not totally unrelated evidence supporting the relative income share hypothesis. For example, resistance to productivity-enhancing techniques coupled with expectations of rising real income causes inflation. Just as human body temperature is a measure of the conflict between invading organisms and the white blood corpuscles, inflation is a measure of the degree of conflict among various special interest groups over the national output. Although inflation lends support to the hypothesis presented in this section, it is essentially a short-run phenomenon. In the long run, the real changes in the economic system occur through substitution and the use of new technologies, the directions of which affect the distributive shares among the groups in conflict.

It was suggested earlier that substitution of factors of production can be viewed as a result of the conflict among the owners of factors of production over the distributive shares of national output. This point needs further elaboration.

THE FACTOR SUBSTITUTION PROCESS

Figure 3.2 shows one possible causal representation of the conflict between capital owners and laborers. As the relative share of income to capital goes down, capital is substituted for labor by increasing the investment in capital. Thus, for a given level of labor input, the capital-to-labor ratio rises with the increase in capital input. Increasing capital intensity, however, has a negative influence on profitability, unless there is a corresponding increase in productivity. When profit rate goes up, the level of investment also increases, and thus adds to the capital stock after a delay. In the figure the income to capital owners is assumed to consist of rentals alone. Thus, for a given rental rate, which is generally stable compared to the wage rate, capital's share of income rises with the

FIGURE 3.2

A Causal Representation of the Conflict between Capital Owners
and Laborers over Distributive Shares of Income

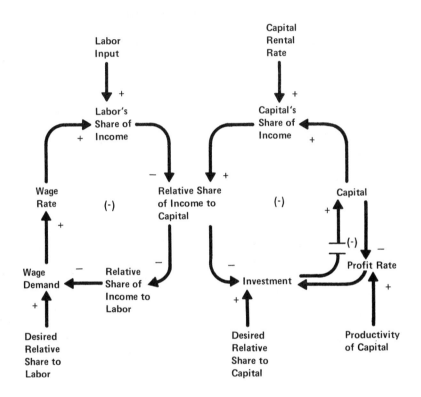

Source: Constructed by the author.

increase in the capital stock. As in the case of capital income, the
relative share of income to labor influences the causal chain of
events represented by the left-hand side of the figure. As the discrepancy between the desired and the actual relative share of income
to labor increases, the demand for higher wages causes the wage
rate to go up. In turn, labor's share of income increases, thereby
causing capital's share of income to fall. Thus, the whole cycle of
events is repeated over and over.

In Figure 3.3 the capital/labor substitution process is shown
more explicitly. Here the negative goal-seeking loop represents the
process by which firms in the economy respond to rises in the wage

FIGURE 3.3

A Causal Representation of the Capital Substitution Process

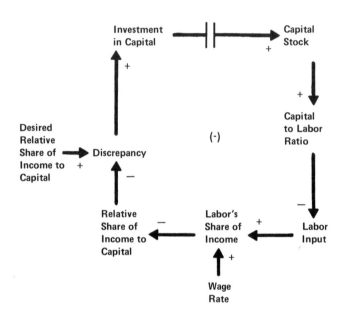

Source: Constructed by the author.

rates. As wage rates rise, the relative share of income to capital goes down and the firms respond by substituting capital for labor.

In the elaboration of capital/labor-substitution process above, it was assumed that there is something known as the desired relative income share against which the actual share is compared to arrive at a sequence of actions. The concept of a desired share needs further consideration. In the neoclassical world of perfect competition and profit maximization, it can be shown that the ratio of income to factors of production would remain constant under equilibrium conditions.[8] Thus, there is an implicit goal of each of the owners of the factors to retain their relative shares of income at a constant level which is also optimal. In contrast, the goal structure of firms in a hypothetical Marxian state would be characterized by zero surplus value or zero profits. In between these two extremes of maximum and zero profits lies the viewpoint that firms are "satisficers."[9]

Since the neoclassical view of firms and markets has already been dismissed as unrealistic, and since the case of the Marxian state is irrelevant, it is useful to consider the case of satisficing firms in detail.

The term satisficing leaves a lot of room for interpretation and thus makes it difficult to develop a precise mathematical model. Nevertheless, elegance of mathematical representation is a poor reason to sacrifice realism in modeling the economic process. In this spirit, one possible interpretation of the goal structure of satisficing firms is presented below.

Consider an economy with a known set of factor shares of output at some arbitrary initial point in time. Assuming that there is no way to know whether the factor shares in this economy represent optimal shares or whether the firms in this economy have realized the maximum possible profits, the only thing that can be said about this economy is that all the participants are reasonably satisfied with their relative shares of output. Now, on the basis of the relative income share hypothesis, it can be stated that all the participants in this economy would resist any reduction in their relative shares of output. The result, in effect, would be a defense of the status quo by the system, even though an individual participant might not be totally happy with his share. Thus, the firms in this economy would be content with a reasonable level of profitability and what is reasonable would be based on what recent history has suggested as achievable. Factors such as fear of adverse public opinion or the possibility of inviting governmental regulation, and so on, tend to determine the upper limit of the desired rate of profitability. Irrespective of what this upper limit might be, there is one thing the satisficing firms would resist—that is, any reduction in their relative share of output. This much information is sufficient to model the domestic production system over the chosen time horizon of 1950 to 2020. During most of this time horizon, U.S. industry has faced or will be facing rising real costs of labor as well as energy. Thus, it seems reasonable to assume that the desired relative share of income to capital is specified by the known initial conditions in the year 1950.

The relative income share hypothesis presented earlier and the interpretation of the factor substitution process presented above are useful in addressing the energy/economy interactions. For example, depletion of conventional resources causes a decline in the productivity of capital and labor in the energy sector of the economy. This leads to a rise in real fuel prices, which in turn leads to a shift in the relative share of income to the energy sector, assuming that the demand for energy is inelastic in the short run. This causes the forces of conservation and substitution to take effect, and hence, oppose the change in order to attain the initial state of distributive shares. This process is represented with the associated time delays in a system dynamic model of the U.S. economy which is presented in Chapter 4.

Besides the dynamic process of factor substitution, it is important to consider the growth in factor productivity which is bound to influence future growth in output. The following section addresses the issue of productivity and presents a hypothesis.

TECHNOLOGY AND PRODUCTIVITY

One of the major factors that have contributed to the historic economic growth in the United States is increase in productivity of factor inputs.[10] Productivity is measured as the output per unit of factor input. Despite its importance in explaining economic growth, there is not a single accepted theory on the determinants of growth in productivity.[11] Empirical investigations suggest various factors responsible for productivity growth—research and development, advances in skill and knowledge of workers, and investment in new capital.[12]

Most recent models of economic growth assume productivity to grow at an exogenously specified rate in the future.† Such an assumption is due partly to the fact that causal factors that influence growth in productivity are not well understood, and partly to a sense of optimism regarding the future. In any case, the assumption lacks a rational basis. In this section, a causal theory on productivity growth is proposed.

All empirical analyses of productivity growth use the statistical approach in identifying the causal factors that affect productivity. In Figure 3.4 the statistical approach to productivity analysis is shown in a schematic form. In using the statistical approach several factors are identified as being independent of each other and their correlations to the growth rate in productivity are determined from regression analyses.[13] These correlations are then used as measures of the relative importance of alternate factors influencing productivity growth.

The use of the statistical approach without a basic causal theory leads to several difficulties in the interpretation of the results. For example, the statistical approach ignores feedback effects and does not provide a framework from which temporal

---

†Both the IEA and the Hudson-Jorgenson models have exogenously specified productivity growth rates.

FIGURE 3.4

A Schematic Representation of the Statistical Analysis
of Productivity Growth

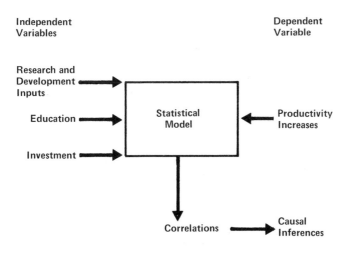

Source: Constructed by the author.

sequence of events, characterized by the independent variables, can
be deduced. As John Kendrick suggests, "In the first place, the theoretical framework itself may be deficient, and fail to specify all
the significant variables, or the correct form of particular variables
with respect to lags, et cetera. Secondly, available econometric
techniques may be inadequate to deal with certain difficult problems,
particularly collinearity reflecting complex interactions among the
independent variables.† Finally, alternative models may produce
equally good results."[14] Due to these difficulties in using the statistical approach to identify the causal sequence of factors that contribute

---

†The collinearity between independent variables in a reasonable
specification is an important issue. The so-called independent variables may not be independent at all. In fact, variables such as research and development inputs and level of education and training of
the labor force are most probably temporally sequentially related.

to a growth in factor productivity, it may be worthwhile to consider the method of a priori reasoning to address the issue of productivity.

Every society noted for its intellectual achievements has allocated, by conscious means or otherwise, a part of its surplus product to the maintenance of its intelligentsia. In modern economies, these allocations take the form of investments in education, research, and development.† Historically such investments, in combination with entrepreneurial talent, led to the development of new techniques of production and distribution that were more efficient than the ones that were being used. The new techniques were efficient in the sense that resource inputs in the process of production were economized. The new techniques were embodied in the new capital goods that were soon introduced into the enterprises of production. A generally competitive environment stimulated the exploitation of new techniques as they became available. The new techniques embodied in capital goods began to create a demand for an increasingly sophisticated labor force. The net result was an increase in both capital and labor productivities which in combination with an increasing demand for goods and services contributed to growth in output. The output in turn led to surpluses that were allocated to research and development. Thus, the whole cycle of causation continued, especially in Western nations, leading to affluence in per capita terms. Figure 3.5 shows a causal representation of the productivity growth process. An important characteristic of the positive feedback loop shown in this figure is perpetual growth.

Does this process of circular positive causation imply continued growth in the future? A simple extrapolation of the past into the future without a reconciliation with nature's immutable law of diminishing returns would be naive. As Alfred Marshall has stated,

> But the world is really a very small place, and there is not room in it for the opening up of rich new resources during many decades at as rapid a rate as has prevailed.

---

†The modern-day example is an act of conscious devotion of resources to encourage research and development in order that the whole society may benefit. In contrast, three centuries ago intellectual indulgence was reserved primarily for the leisure class; and the leisure class consisted of the aristocracy and the clergy. In this case, the social arrangements permitted a few to pursue research and development and as such it was not a conscious act on the part of the society. The afforded leisure, in combination with other unique cultural traits, led to the development of new techniques of production.

FIGURE 3.5

A Causal Representation of the Productivity Growth Process

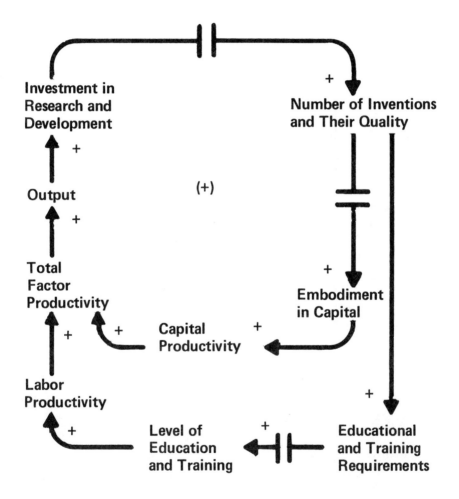

FIGURE 3.6

A Causal Diagram Illustrating Diminishing Returns in Productivity

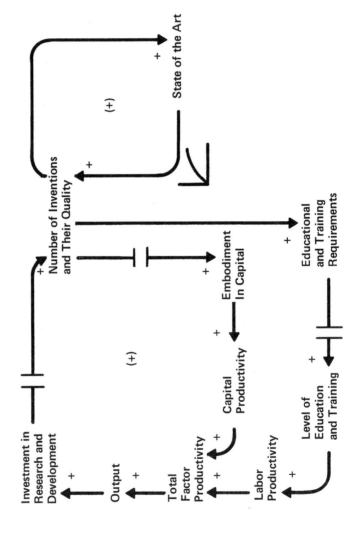

Source: Constructed by the author.

34

. . . When new countries begin to need most of their own food and other raw produce, improvements in transport will count for little. From that time onward the pressure of the Law of Diminishing Return can be opposed only by further improvements in production; and improvements in production themselves gradually show a diminishing return. [15]

What Marshall is suggesting is that the means of producing the basic goods and services that are essential for human survival cannot improve in efficiency indefinitely. The implication of Marshall's suggestion is incorporated in Figure 3.6. As the number of inventions and their productive quality increase, the state of the art, which could be measured by the cumulative value of all the inventions in a specific area of production, becomes increasingly saturated and gradually limits further gains in productive quality. The right-hand side positive feedback loop in Figure 3.6 has a continuously declining gain. A good example that would support Marshall's statement is the historical gains made in the heat rate in steam-electric power plants which reached a saturation point in the late 1950s. [16] Marshall's hypothesis essentially challenges the notion that human ability to invent and innovate is limitless. [17]

Before proceeding to test the empirical validity of Marshall's statement, it is necessary to restate the hypothesis regarding productivity in more precise terms. A precise statement of hypothesis must precede empirical observations. As Jay Forrester suggests, ". . . before we measure, we should name the quantity, select a scale of measurement, and in the interests of efficiency we should have a reason for wanting to know." [18] In the next section one such statement is provided and its implications elaborated.

THE PRODUCTIVITY HYPOTHESIS

In a modern industrial economy, the means of satisfying the demand for a product through the system of production and distribution improve in efficiency or productivity with investments in research and development and with the embodiment of new techniques in the factors of production. The improvements in productivity obey the law of diminishing returns to cumulative inputs in research and development.

The statement above consists of two major propositions. The first one implies that a product for which a demand exists is produced by firms by means of employment of the factors of production such as capital and labor. And the productivity of these factors improves with systematic investments in research and development. There are several studies that confirm this first proposition (see Note 10).

The second proposition suggests that there are diminishing returns to cumulative investments in research and development. There is an important reason for considering the cumulative investments rather than the current inputs: at every instant a society benefits from the knowledge of techniques of production and distribution that was generated in the past. Each generation passes on a cumulative stock of knowledge to posterity. Without this intergenerational transfer of knowledge the survival of societies would have been severely impaired. For instance, the invention of the wheel has benefited mankind in countless ways, and, to the extent that the present generation does not have to invent the wheel, it enjoys the benefits of prehistoric labor. Of course, the wheel has undergone many technical changes that have reduced frictional losses; but the basic concept remains the same and any new improvements of the wheel most certainly have not had the same degree of contribution to human welfare as the invention of the wheel itself. Similarly, Newton's laws of motion have aided engineering designers for over two centuries. The benefits of the resources devoted by seventeenth-century England to the support of Newton and his work have been reaped by every modern industrialized society.

The point is that modern industrialized nations enjoy the benefits of the cumulative value of resources devoted to research and development by societies in the past. Moreover, knowledge, unlike physical capital, does not depreciate with use. Rather, it is gained through innumerable trials and errors, and both the trials and the errors contribute to the sum total of knowledge of value to the future generations. Thus, it seems reasonable to assume that the rate of new additions to useful knowledge is determined by the level of cumulative resources devoted to research and development, at any point in time.

Now, if it is further assumed that with time the market basket of goods demanded by a society becomes invariant in composition, then the means of providing the goods must reach a level of saturation in efficiency. Food, fuel, shelter, mobility, and health care are some of the basic human needs. The means of satisfying these needs do not change overnight. It may take centuries for human beings to abandon the concept of food derived from organic matter and substitute synthetics totally. Moreover, the green revolution in food production is based on unsustainable methods of capital and energy-intensive agriculture.[19] As energy becomes increasingly expensive the agricultural productivity is bound to suffer significantly. Furthermore, finite resources such as air and water are no longer considered available for use free of charges. Thus, the emerging concern over environmental quality and safety at the place of work is already having a negative influence on productivity.[20] These emerging trends seem to confirm the concept of diminishing returns in productivity growth.

Figure 3.7 shows a causal representation of the productivity hypothesis. The relationship between the cumulative investments in research and development and factor productivity is specified by the nonlinear function indicated beside the causal link connecting these two variables. This function implies that the law of diminishing returns applies to the relationship between these two factors.

Intuitively, it would seem that since each generation adds to the existing stock of knowledge of production techniques, the knowledge must grow exponentially. This may be true, but empirical evidence suggests that this seemingly explosive growth in knowledge has not added proportionately to productivity growth. In Figures 3.8 through 3.11 the productivity indexes for four energy-intensive primary production sectors of the U.S. economy are plotted against the cumulative value of research and development expenditures. Historical data on research and development expenditures for individual sectors were not available for the period before 1950. Luckily, this is not a serious problem, since the diminishing-returns hypothesis would be obeyed regardless of the choice of initial time period, as can be seen from these figures. These plots were made from time-series data for the period between 1950 and 1970. A shortcoming in the present consideration is that diffusion of technology from other sectors was not taken into account. Such an accounting would not change the basic trend that has emerged historically, since accounting for diffusion would add only to the abscissa. Further, productivity is not represented here as a delayed function of research inputs, since it would not change the basic trend of diminishing returns. Thus, though these plots should be viewed merely as illustrations of the diminishing-returns hypothesis, they do tentatively suggest that there is sufficient reason to believe in the validity of the hypothesis.

A logical application of the diminishing-returns hypothesis suggests that it is very likely that the productivity growth in these four representative sectors of the economy will be saturated by the turn of the century. Given the rising concern over environment and safety, it may be that saturation will occur within the next decade.

In analyzing the growth in factor productivity so far, the random occurrences of technological breakthroughs have not been taken into account. History indicates that many of the breakthroughs have occurred in a random manner, and it would have been difficult to predict their nature. It should be noted that many technologies that

FIGURE 3.7

A Causal Representation of the Productivity Growth Hypothesis

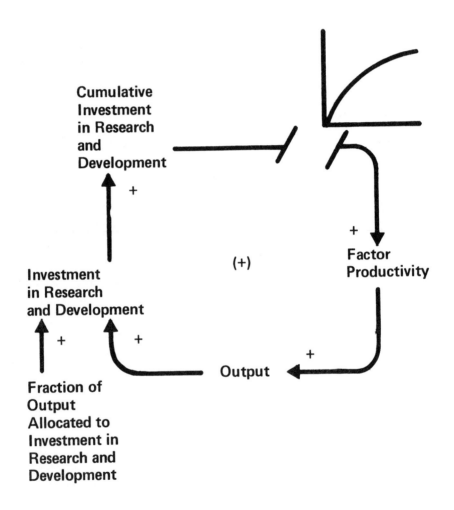

Source: Constructed by the author.

FIGURE 3.8

Productivity Trends in the U.S. Primary Metals Sector

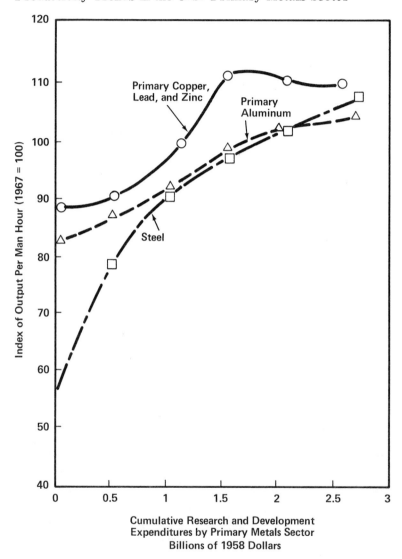

Note: The current dollar research and development expenditures were converted to constant 1958 dollars using the GNP service sector deflators.

Source: U.S. Bureau of the Census, Historical Statistics of the United States, Colonial Times to 1970 (Washington, D.C., 1976), pp. 951, 966, 967.

FIGURE 3.9

Productivity Trends in the U.S. Food and Kindred Products Sector

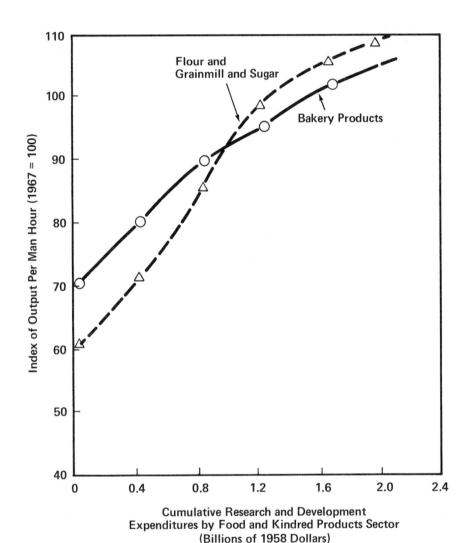

Source: U.S. Bureau of the Census, Historical Statistics of the United States, Colonial Times to 1970 (Washington, D.C., 1976), pp. 950, 966-67.

FIGURE 3.10

Productivity Trends in the U.S. Farm Sector

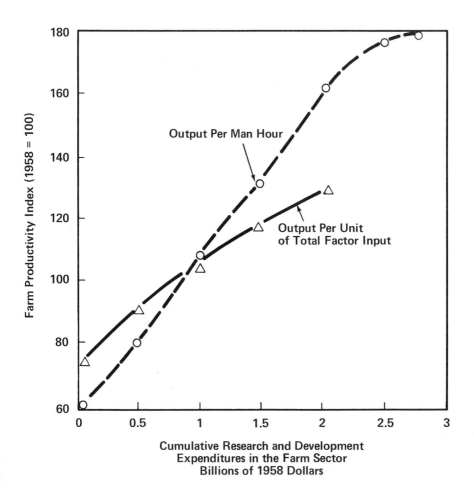

Source: U.S. Bureau of the Census, Historical Statistics of the United States, Colonial Times to 1970 (Washington, D.C., 1976), pp. 197, 966.

FIGURE 3.11

Productivity Trend in the U.S. Chemical and Allied Products Sector

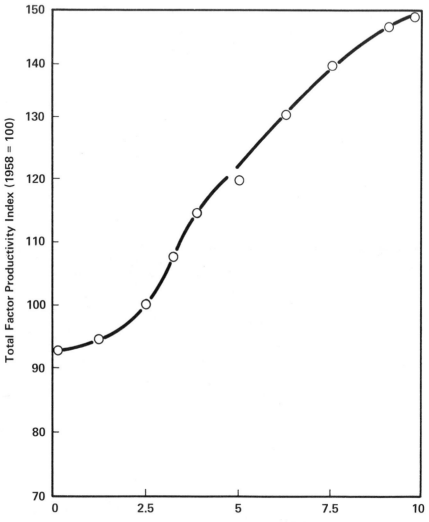

Cumulative Research and Development
Expenditure by Chemical and Allied Products Sector
(Billions of 1958 Dollars)

Sources: U.S. Bureau of the Census, Historical Statistics of the United States, Colonial Times to 1970 (Washington, D.C., 1976), pp. 966-67; John W. Kendrick, Postwar Productivity Trends in the United States, 1948-1969 (New York: National Bureau of Economic Research, 1973), p. 301.

were at first considered miracles are now being branded as curses. Thus, history provides a basis for neither optimism nor pessimism in speculating about future possibilities.[21] It is quite likely, given the historical record, that new technologies will emerge in the future as a response to increasing pressures on the earth's resources. At this point in time, it is virtually impossible to foretell the direction or the nature of future technical changes. Already there are suggestions for colonizing outer space and the ocean depths. Thus, due to the very nature of technological progress, it becomes necessary to construct a model of economic growth through which alternate assumptions can be easily tested. The model presented in Chapter 4 is designed to allow such a testing of alternate possible hypotheses.

One of the major implications of the possible decline in productivity growth is that demand for investment in capital goods may decline due to diminishing returns, assuming that population does not continue to grow at the historical rates. This point calls for a description of the behavioral factors influencing the investment decision in the economy.

SAVINGS AND INVESTMENT

In this section the standard-price theory of savings and investment is discussed, and the difficulties of using such a theory in a disequilibrium model of the economy are identified.

The standard-price theory views savings as the amount of current output deferred for consumption in the future. Savings help finance the formation of new capital and the replacement of depreciated machinery and structures. The allocation of savings in the capital formation process is termed investment, which is an important determinant of economic growth.[22] Also, substitution of capital for labor requires investment in new capital, as discussed in an earlier section of this chapter.

In analyzing the energy/economy interactions there is a need for representing the capital accumulation process within the structure of the model of the economy. The savings rate, which is the fraction of output not allocated for investment, determines the limiting rate at which capital can accumulate. And the investment allocation into the energy sector and the rest of the economy determines the limiting rates at which capital accumulates within each of these sectors. Since the limiting rate of capital accumulation governs the growth rates of output and energy use, it is necessary to represent this rate-constraining process in a model of energy/economy interactions.

FIGURE 3.12

A Causal Representation of the Savings and Investment Process

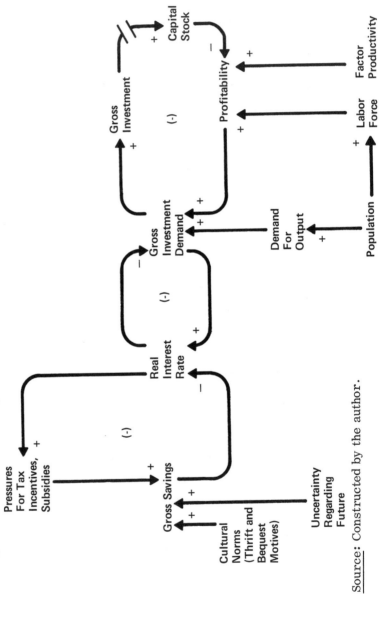

Source: Constructed by the author.

The price theory† suggests that the factors that govern the savings rate are different from those that govern the demand for investment. The savings rate is a function of cultural norms such as thrift and bequest motives, concern for the future such as the retirement years, and simply the desire to accumulate wealth, whereas investment demand is a function of profitable opportunities that may exist in the production of goods and services. The real interest rate, which is determined by the supply of savings and the demand for investment, is analogous to price as a balancing mechanism, as in the case of basic commodities.‡ Price theory assumes that perfect competition exists in the capital markets where savings and investments are matched for a given real interest rate. An implication of the perfect competition assumption is that investors, who desire to maximize their returns, will allocate their savings in such a manner that at the end of the allocation process, the marginal efficiency of all the capital assets will equal the real interest rate.

Figure 3.12 shows a simplified causal representation of the savings and investment process, as viewed by the price theory. In this figure, there are three negative feedback loops, representing the savings, the investment, and the capital accumulation processes, respectively. The savings loop, on the extreme left-hand side of the figure, includes the role played by government in the savings process.

Strictly speaking, price theory does not include government as a saver. Only households and firms contribute to national savings. But in a mixed economy government plays a major role in the savings and investment process through subsidies and taxes. Furthermore, government can influence the savings rate in a negative manner through deficits, which must be financed in the open market. The inclusion of this factor is mainly to suggest that government, through its power to subsidize capital formation, plays a significant role in the savings process. However, if it is assumed that government actions are only a minor part of the whole savings process, then the perfect market assumption of price theory stands as a valid one. Then, the representation of the price-theoretic viewpoint of the savings and investment process, as shown in Figure 3.12, seems accurate.

As the demand for investment rises, the real interest rate rises, stimulating additional savings. At the same time the demand

---

†For lack of a better term, standard economic theory is denoted as price theory.[23]

‡Here real interest rate is used in the sense that the rate is inflation-adjusted money interest rate.

for investment is tempered by the rising interest rate. The savings are then invested in various forms of capital according to their relative profitabilities. Thus, as the gross investment demand rises, the actual investments eventually increase, as shown in the right-hand loop. This adds to the capital stock after a delay. As the capital stock increases it has a depressing effect on the profitability for a given level of productivity and the labor force, due to the law of diminishing returns. However, an increase in productivity, due to the employment of new and sophisticated capital goods, opposes the negative effect of capital on profitability. As profitability increases, it creates additional demand for investment for a given level of interest rate, which in turn stimulates savings. The whole process outlined above repeats until an equilibrium is reached. Under equilibrium conditions, the profit rate at the margin will equal the real interest rate. Such is the nature of the free-market adjustment process. It is generally assumed, in price theory, that the adjustment-time constants are small enough to view the savings and investment process as an essentially simultaneous event. Thus, savings and investment by definition must always be equal, as viewed by price theory.

Although price theory provides a useful description of the savings and investment process, it is difficult to use this theory in a disequilibrium model of the economy. For instance, empirical evidence suggests that the causal link between the real interest rate and the savings rate is extremely weak.[24] Moreover, it has been observed that the savings rate in the United States has been relatively stable for a long time, despite the fluctuations in the interest rates.[25] Many recent studies of long-term capital availability in the United States have assumed that the savings rate will remain constant in the future.[26] Such an assumption has led to certain recent debates over the adequacy of domestic savings in the future to meet the rising investment demands created by concerns about energy self-sufficiency, environment, safety, and health.[27] These debates implicitly raise important questions regarding the usefulness of price theory as a descriptive view of the functioning of domestic capital markets. The problem is that price theory applies only to a hypothetical economy where perfect markets with instantaneous adjustment processes exist. There is one major premise on which the price theory could be criticized.

The relative insensitivity of savings rate to changes in interest rates implies either that the causal link between interest rate and savings rate is nonexistent or that there may be a long delay between these two variables. If the latter is true, then it can be shown that the price theory would lead to absurd results in a disequilibrium model. In a disequilibrium situation, the savings rate and the invest-

FIGURE 3.13

A Disequilibrium Representation of the Savings and Investment
Process

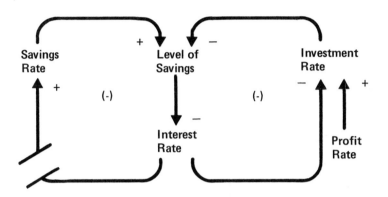

Source: Constructed by the author.

ment rate must interact through an intermediate level or a state
variable. For convenience this is called the volume of savings,
which is analogous to inventories in commodity systems. The volume of savings increases with the savings rate and depletes with
investment rate as shown in Figure 3.13. Now if, for some reason
such as capital deepening, the demand for investment drops, then
there will be an excess of savings at least for some period of time,
due to the long delay that has been assumed for savings rate to
adjust to changes in the interest rate. But an excess of savings has
no meaning in the real world, unless one includes hoarding as a
part of savings. Price theory, however, requires that at the end of
each period savings rate and investment rate must be equal. This
is clearly impossible in a disequilibrium situation. Thus the need
for an alternate hypothesis on the savings and investment process
clearly emerges.

One of the major difficulties in using the price theory to model
the disequilibrium effects in capital markets is that there is no
identifiable stock variable corresponding to inventories in commodity
markets. One way to get around this problem is to reject the dis-
tinction between savings and investment as two separate variables.
As Joseph Schumpeter suggests,

Normally people save with a view to some return, in
money or in services of some "investment good." It is
not only that the bulk of individual savings—and of
course, practically all business savings which, in turn,
constitute the greater part of total saving—is done with
a specific investment purpose in view. The decision to
invest precedes as a rule, and the act of investing precedes very often, the decision to save. Even in those
cases in which a man saves without specific investment
purpose, any delay in coming to an investment decision
is punished by the loss of return for the interval. It
seems to follow, first, that unless people see investment
opportunities, they will not normally save and the situation of vanishing investment opportunity is likely to be
also one of vanishing saving. [28]

A major implication of Schumpeter's statement is that the act
of saving is a consequence of the existence of opportunities for
investment. In this light, the historical constancy of the savings
rate could be viewed as constancy of investment opportunities. In
other words, all the investment opportunities with a promise of
some reasonable profitability were exploited in the past, and it is
just a coincidence that the investment rate was invariant. Therefore, it may be that in the future investment (savings) rate will
change from its historical constancy, depending on the availability
of profitable investment opportunities. Furthermore, in the past it
was not only the savings decisions that were insensitive to changes
in the interest rates, but also investment decisions, since the
decision to invest must precede the decision to save, according to
Schumpeter. Thus, it seems reasonable to reject not only the concept of savings as an independent variable, but also the concept of
the real interest rate as a balancing mechanism. The real interest
rate could be replaced by the concept of desired profitability which
was discussed in an earlier section on factor substitution.

In that discussion it was stated that the present study assumes
the U.S. economy to consist of satisficing rather than maximizing
firms. It was argued that the satisficing firms base their decisions
on reasonable profitability—a concept that is imbedded in every
decision-making unit in the domestic economy. This is apparent
from the fact that there are frequently public outcries against
"obscene" profits. Evidently, if a certain profit rate is obscene
then there must be a concept of reasonable profitability. As was
argued before, one possible interpretation of reasonable profit rate
could be to consider the actual realized average profit rates

FIGURE 3.14

A Causal Representation of the Savings and Investment Hypothesis

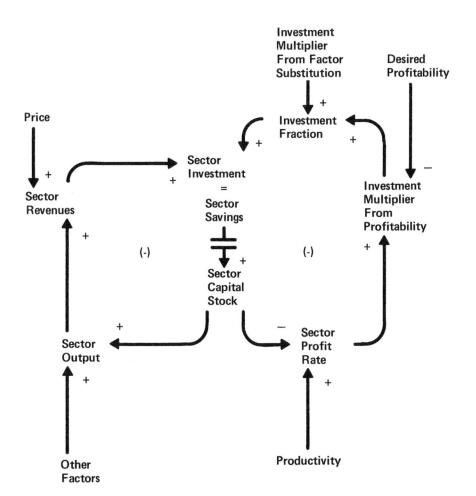

Source: Constructed by the author.

historically. Using this concept of reasonable profitability, a descriptive hypothesis of the savings and investment process can be stated.

THE SAVINGS AND INVESTMENT HYPOTHESIS

A modern industrial economy such as the United States consists of satisficing firms which exploit all the investment opportunities that promise a reasonable level of profitability. This concept of reasonable profitability, which is based on historical average of realized profit rates, changes slowly over time. Further, the sum total of the investments of all firms constitutes, ex post, the national savings.

Figure 3.14 is a causal diagram of the investment hypothesis, representing the implication of the hypothesis for a single sector of the economy, such as the energy industry. As the sector capital stock increases, the sector profit rate declines, ceteris paribus. If the profit rate is greater than a desired (reasonable) rate, then the sector invests until the discrepancy between the desired rate and the actual rate is zero. The limiting rate at which capital is accumulated by a sector is specified by the investment fraction. The investment fraction itself is a function of investment multipliers from the factor substitution process (see Figure 3.2) and profitability. As argued earlier, the investment multiplier from factor substitution is based on the conflict among factors of production to maintain the relative shares of output. In contrast, the multiplier from profitability depends on the realized profit rate, which in turn depends on the productivity of factor inputs.

The savings and investment hypothesis described above should be viewed merely as a tentative one that allows a simple representation of the savings/investment process in a model economy. Due to the complexity of the functioning of capital markets in this country, and for a lack of a better theory, a simple abstraction of reality is outlined here. Developing an alternative to the price theory itself may be a separate area of research, and a need for such a project is clear.

In the following chapter, the three hypotheses outlined in this chapter are incorporated within the formal structure of a macroeconomic model of the U.S. economy.

NOTES

1. James S. Duesenberry, Income, Saving, and the Theory of Consumer Behavior (New York: Oxford University Press, 1967), pp. 45-46.

2. Nicholas Georgescu-Roegen, The Entropy Law and the Economic Process (Cambridge, Mass.: Harvard University Press, 1971), pp. 319-20.

3. Alfred E. Kahn, "Market Power Inflation—A Conceptual Overview," in The Roots of Inflation, ed. John M. Blair (New York: Burt Franklin, 1975), p. 271.

4. See William C. Mitchell, "The Shape of Political Theory to Come—From Political Sociology to Political Economy," in Politics and the Social Sciences, ed. Seymour Martin Lipset (Oxford: Oxford University Press, 1969), p. 114.

5. For a description of the zero-sum game, see John Von Neumann and Oskar Morgenstern, Theory of Games and Economic Behavior (New York: Wiley, 1964), pp. 85-165.

6. Kahn, "Market Power Inflation," p. 269.

7. C. C. von Weizsäcker, "Notes on Endogenous Growth of Productivity," in Models of Economic Growth, ed. James A. Mirrlees and N. H. Stern (New York: Wiley, 1973), p. 110.

8. See R. G. D. Allen, Mathematical Analysis for Economists (New York: St. Martin's Press, 1938), p. 364.

9. See Herbert A. Simon, Administrative Behavior (New York: Macmillan, 1961), pp. 61-109. Simon coined the term "satisficers" to represent the suboptimal decision makers who manage the firms.

10. For examples of empirical analysis, see Edward Denison, Accounting for United States Economic Growth, 1929-1969 (Washington, D.C.: The Brookings Institution, 1974); and John W. Kendrick, Postwar Productivity Trends in the United States, 1948-1969 (New York: National Bureau of Economic Research, 1973). For a useful discussion on the role of technology, see Nathan Rosenberg, Perspectives on Technology (Cambridge: Cambridge University Press, 1976).

11. For a theoretical treatment of the role of technology, see Murray Brown, ed., The Theory and Empirical Analysis of Production (New York: National Bureau of Economic Research, 1967); and B. R. Williams, ed., Science and Technology in Economic Growth (New York: Wiley, 1973).

12. See Griliches, "Research Expenditures and Growth Accounting," in Williams, Science and Technology in Economic Growth, pp. 59-83; and N. E. Terleckyj, Effects of R & D on the Productivity Growth of Industries (Washington, D.C.: National Planning Associates, 1974).

13. For a description of the statistical approach generally used in productivity analyses, see J. Johnston, Econometric Methods (New York: McGraw-Hill, 1963).

14. Kendrick, Postwar Productivity Trends in the United States, p. 134.

15. A. C. Pigou, Memorials of Alfred Marshall (London: Macmillan, 1925), p. 326. Also quoted in Harold J. Barnett and Chandler Morse, Scarcity and Growth (Baltimore: Johns Hopkins University Press, 1963), p. 236.

16. See, for example, M. Granger Morgan, ed., Energy and Man: Technical and Social Aspects of Energy (New York: IEEE Press, 1975), p. 237.

17. Some recent authors have questioned the assumption of limitless capacity for invention and innovation on the part of human beings. For example, see E. F. Schumacher, Small is Beautiful— Economics as if People Mattered (New York: Harper and Row, 1973), p. 147.

18. Jay W. Forrester, Industrial Dynamics (Cambridge, Mass.: MIT Press, 1961), p. 59.

19. See Barry Commoner, The Closing Circle (New York: Knopf, 1971) for an analysis of many such technology-related problems.

20. See, for example, Gordon F. Bloom, "Productivity: Weak Link in our Economy," Harvard Business Review 49 (January/February 1971): 4.

21. Commoner, The Closing Circle.

22. For a discussion on this point, see Daniel Hamberg, Models of Economic Growth (New York: Harper and Row, 1971), pp. 141-99.

23. For a basic description of the standard theory, see Paul A. Samuelson, Economics (New York: McGraw-Hill, 1973), pp. 205-19.

24. See, for example, Duesenberry, Income, Saving, and the Theory of Consumer Behavior, p. 45; and Robin Barlow, Harvey Brazer, and James Morgan, Economic Behavior of the Affluent (Washington, D.C.: The Brookings Institution, 1966), p. 85.

25. See Simon Kuznets, Capital in the American Economy— Its Formation and Financing (Princeton, N.J.: Princeton University Press, 1961), pp. 91-109; and Duesenberry, Income, Saving, and the Theory of Consumer Behavior, pp. 39-41.

26. New York Stock Exchange, The Capital Needs and Savings Potential of the U.S. Economy, Projections Through 1985 (New York: NYSE, 1974); and Barry Bosworth, James Duesenberry, and Andrew Carron, Capital Needs in the Seventies (Washington, D.C.: The Brookings Institution, 1975). Also, the IEA study reviewed in Chapter 2 assumes a constant savings rate.

27. For a review of capital availability debates, see Robert Eisner, "The Outlook for Business Investment," in Capital for Productivity and Jobs, The American Assembly, Columbia University (Englewood Cliffs, N.J.: Prentice-Hall, 1977), pp. 50-72; Solomon Fabricant, "Perspective on Capital Requirements Question," in

Capital for Productivity and Jobs, pp. 27-49; Leonall C. Anderson, "Is There a Capital Shortage: Theory and Recent Empirical Evidence," Journal of Finance 31 (May 1976): 257-68; Paul Wachtel, Arnold Sametz, and Harry Schuford, "Capital Shortages: Myth or Reality?," Journal of Finance 31 (May 1976): 269-86; and Andrew Brimmer and Allen Sinai, "The Effects of Tax Policy on Capital Formation, Corporate Liquidity, and the Availability of Investible Funds: A Simulation Study," Journal of Finance 31 (May 1976): 287-308. For a review of capital availability for the energy sector, see Jerome Hass, Edward Mitchell, and Bernell Stone, Financing the Energy Industry, Ford Foundation Report (Cambridge, Mass.: Ballinger, 1974).

28. Joseph Schumpeter, Capitalism, Socialism, and Democracy (New York: Harper and Row, 1942), p. 395.

4

THE ECONOMY1 MODEL

INTRODUCTION

The ECONOMY1 model is designed to analyze the long-term dynamic interactions between the energy sector and the rest of the economy of the United States. There are two major interactions represented in the model. The first is due to energy shortages that cause a reduction in the utilization of the factors of production, and the second is due to rising energy prices that cause transfer of income from the rest of the economy to the energy sector. These interactions are described in detail in this chapter.

The energy production sector is represented by a system dynamics model known as FOSSIL1,[1] and the rest of the economy is represented by the ECONOMY1 model.[†] The FOSSIL1 model requires net energy demand as input, and generates the level of prices and

---

[†]The original version of the FOSSIL1 model includes the price feedback on energy demand endogenously, and GNP is exogenous to the model. The original version was modified to interact with ECONOMY1 by incorporating the price effects in the ECONOMY1 model.

Throughout the present chapter the system dynamics notations are used in describing the structure and the equations of the model. This method uses a set of coupled, nonlinear, ordinary differential equations in representing the structure of the model system. Furthermore, these equations are solved by using a DYNAMO compiler which uses the Euler numerical integration technique. The DYNAMO equations consist of notations of variables according to whether

FIGURE 4.1

The Interactions between ECONOMY1 and FOSSIL1

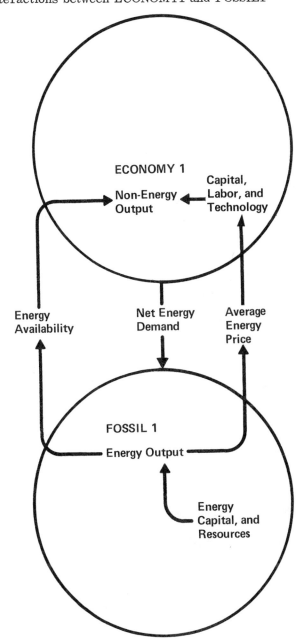

Source: Constructed by the author.

outputs of coal, oil, natural gas, electricity, and synthetic fuels. The ECONOMY1 model requires net energy availability and the net average energy price as inputs, and generates the level of nonenergy output in the economy. An overall view of these interactions is shown in Figure 4.1.

A brief description of the FOSSIL1 model is provided here, followed by a detailed description of the U.S. economy, as depicted by the ECONOMY1 model.

THE FOSSIL1 MODEL

The FOSSIL1 model, designed to represent in detail the U.S. energy production system, consists of the following five sectors: the inter-fuel substitution sector, † the coal sector, the oil sector, the gas sector, and the electricity sector.

Given a net energy demand for the whole economy, the inter-fuel substitution sector is designed to find end-use demands for coal, oil, gas, and electricity. These end-use demands are determined within the model as a function of relative fuel prices, availability, and relative convenience. The end-use demands are input to the four energy production sectors as indicated in Figure 4.2.

The energy production sectors in FOSSIL1 are designed to capture the decision processes of the respective energy industries in the United States. These decision processes are, in general, based on the interactions among production capacity, output, and the level of resources. For example, a typical decision would be to expand production capacity. Such a decision is represented in the model as a function of returns to invested capital at the margin. The returns, in turn, depend on fuel price and the marginal cost of production. The marginal cost is determined in the model as a function of the level of resources that remain to be exploited.

---

they are stock or flow variables. For example, if $dY/dt = F(Y)$ is the differential equation, then Y is termed the "level" variable, dY/dt is termed the "rate" variable, and the function "F" is any non-linear combination of variables generally known as "auxiliaries" and "constants."[2]

†In the original version of FOSSIL1, the interfuel substitution sector was an integral part of the demand sector. The present description, however, relates to a modified version of the demand sector of FOSSIL1. The ECONOMY1 model takes the place of the demand sector in the original version.

FIGURE 4.2

The Major Sectors in the FOSSIL1 Model

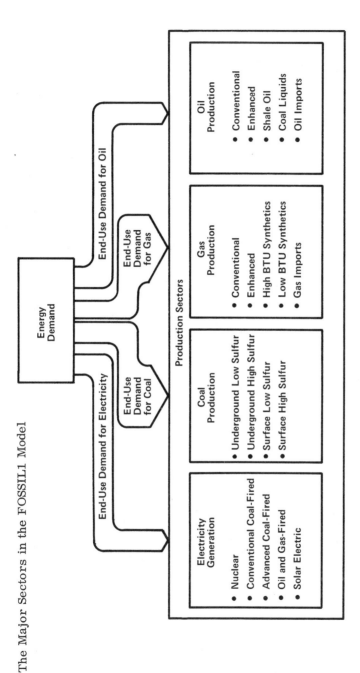

Source: "FOSSIL1 Documentation," Dartmouth System Dynamics Group, Thayer School of Engineering, Dartmouth College, Hanover, New Hampshire, p. 3.

TABLE 4.1

Policy Options in the FOSSIL1 Model

	Oil	Gas	Electricity	Coal	Demand
ERDA policies	1. Accelerated RD&D in Enhanced Oil Recovery 2. Accelerated RD&D in Oil Shale 3. Accelerated RD&D in Coal Liquefaction	1. Accelerated RD&D in Enhanced Gas Recovery 2. Accelerated RD&D in Low-Btu Gas 3. Accelerated RD&D in High-Btu Gas	1. Accelerated RD&D in Atmospheric Coal Combustion 2. Accelerated RD&D in Pressurized Coal Combustion 3. Accelerated RD&D in Combined Cycle Coal Combustion 4. Accelerated RD&D in Advanced Coal Combustion	1. Accelerated RD&D in Coal Beneficiation	1. Accelerated RD&D in Coal End-Use Technologies
Government (non-ERDA) policies	1. Oil Import Tariff 2. Oil Import Quota 3. Total Oil Deregulation 4. Phased Oil Deregulation 5. Price Supports for Oil Shale 6. Price Supports for Coal Liquefaction 7. Price Supports for Oil Synthetics 8. Loan Guarantees for Oil Shale 9. Loan Guarantees for Coal Liquefaction 10. Loan Guarantees for Oil Synthetics 11. Price Supports/Loan Guarantees for Oil Synthetics 12. Accelerated Coal Liquefaction Facility Construction 13. Accelerated Shale Oil Facility Construction 14. Accelerated Synthetic Oil Facility Construction	1. Gas Import Tariff 2. Gas Import Quotas 3. Total Gas Deregulation 4. Phased Gas Deregulation 5. Price Supports for High-Btu Gas 6. Price Supports for Low-Btu Gas 7. Price Supports for Gas Synthetics 8. Loan Guarantees for High-Btu Gas 9. Loan Guarantees for Low-Btu Gas 10. Loan Guarantees for Gas Synthetics 11. Price Supports/Loan Guarantees for Gas Synthetics 12. Accelerated High-Btu Gas Facility Construction 13. Accelerated Low-Btu Gas Facility Construction 14. Accelerated Synthetic Gas Facility Construction	1. Rate Relief 2. Load Management 3. Nuclear Moratorium 4. Breeder Moratorium 5. Postponed Nuclear Fuel Reprocessing 6. Ban on Plutonium Recycle 7. Accelerated Nuclear Facility Construction 8. Relaxation of SO_2 Standards 9. Moratorium on Oil- and Gas-Fired Utilities 10. Ban on Utility Gas Use 11. Moratorium on Non-Emission Controlled Coal Plants	1. Ban on Steep-Slope Mining 2. Ban on Surface Mining 3. Coal Severance Tax 4. Surface Coal Reclamation Standards 5. Stricter Underground Mining Safety Standards	1. Conservation Measures 2. Oil Excise Tax 3. Gas Excise Tax 4. Energy Tax 5. Accelerated Coal Conversion in Industry
Alternative Scenarios	1. OPEC Oil Embargo 2. Exogenous OPEC Pricing Scheme 3. Accelerated OPEC Capacity Expansion Program	1. OPEC Gas Embargo	1. Nuclear Fuel Exports	1. Accelerated Coal Exports	

Source: "FOSSIL1 Technical Appendices," Dartmouth System Dynamics Group, Thayer School of Engineering, Dartmouth College, Hanover, New Hampshire, p. 9.

The FOSSIL1 model has, incorporated within its structure, policy variables to aid in the testing of alternate governmental policy options, such as deregulation of natural gas price and loan guarantees for the use of new technologies for coal conversion. A list of potential options that could be tested with the aid of the FOSSIL1 model is given in Table 4.1.[3]

THE ECONOMY1 MODEL DESCRIPTION

The ECONOMY1 model is a highly aggregated macroeconomic representation of the U.S. economy exclusive of the energy production sector. The model is designed to capture the decision processes of the energy-consuming sectors of the domestic economy. These decision processes involve responses to shortages of fuel and the average energy price.

For the sake of convenience, the ECONOMY1 model is divided into the following seven sectors: the population and labor-force sector, the labor productivity and wages sector, the nonenergy production sector, the product and income share accounting sector, the factor substitution and investment sector, the energy demand sector, and the technology sector. Figure 4.3 shows a causal representation of the interactions among these seven sectors. The heavy connecting lines in the diagram are used to emphasize the important feedback mechanisms incorporated within the structure of the ECONOMY1 model. The top outer loop indicates the capital accumulation and the growth process. The gain of this positive feedback loop is influenced by an income deflator mechanism which is a function of the energy price. The deflator variable is used in the model to combine the monetary flows in the energy sector and the rest of the economy in terms of constant 1975 dollar flows. Through the deflator mechanism in the model, for example, the rising real price of energy can reduce the growth in nonenergy capital by reducing the returns to capital, which causes a reduction in the fraction of output allocated to investment.

The bottom loop in Figure 4.3 represents the substitution or conservation process whereby the demand for energy is reduced as a response to the rising price of energy. The energy availability effect is represented by the capacity utilization variable in the bottom loop. This variable is a function of the energy demand and the actual energy available for consumption. Thus, in case of energy

FIGURE 4.3

A Causal Representation of the ECONOMY1 Model

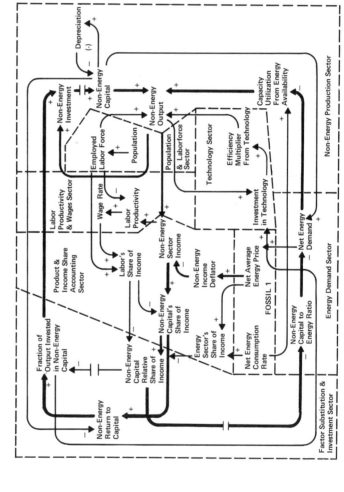

Source: Constructed by the author.

60

shortages, the gain of the growth loop is affected by reduced non-energy output due to reduced capacity utilization.†

With the aid of the two major feedback loops (the top and the bottom loops shown in Figure 4.3 by heavy lines) the normal economic growth process and the effect on growth due to energy prices and energy shortages are represented within the structure of the ECONOMY1 model. These effects are treated in detail with several illustrative model runs at the end of this chapter.

Appendix B shows a DYNAMO flow diagram of the ECONOMY1 model, which explicitly indicates the interactions among variables, rate variables, auxiliaries, and constants.[4] This diagram is useful in tracing through the logical structure of the model.

In the following sections the individual model sectors are described and the associated DYNAMO equations are presented. In addition, the estimations of model parameters are included in the description of each of the sectors.

The Population and Labor-Force Sector

In ECONOMY1 the level of population determines the level of the labor force available for the production of nonenergy goods and services. Population is specified exogenously as a time-dependent function in the model. Table 4.2 shows three different projections of population by the Bureau of the Census. The medium case was chosen as a reference input to the ECONOMY1 model. A user of the model is free to alter this assumption by changing the table function relationship POPT shown in Figure 4.4. The DYNAMO equations‡ representing the population assumption are given below.

---

†Net energy demand is the amount of energy demanded by final consumers, and gross energy demand includes the conversion losses in electricity production. A shortage in energy availability occurs when there is positive discrepancy between net energy demanded for end-use and the net energy supplied by producers at a given price.

‡The author assumes the reader is familiar with DYNAMO equation notations. The number in the right hand side of the equation is provided for cross-reference with the corresponding variable in the DYNAMO flow diagram shown in Appendix B to this volume. For an explanation of the notations, see Alexander Pugh III, DYNA-MO II User's Manual, 4th ed. (Cambridge, Mass.: MIT Press, 1973).

TABLE 4.2

Bureau of the Census Population Projections
(in millions)

Year	Series I High	Series II Medium	Series III Low
1950	152		
1960	181		
1970	205		
1980	226	223	220
1990	258	245	237
2000	287	262	245
2010	322	279	250
2020	362	294	252

Source: U.S. Bureau of the Census, Statistical
Abstracts of the United States (Washington, D.C.,
1976), p. 8.

POP.K = TABHL(POPT, TIME.K, 1950, 2020, 10)*1E8   1.0 A

POPT = 1.52/1.81/2.05/2.23/2.45/2.62/2.79/2.94   1.1 T

where

POP   = population (people)
TABHL = tabular relationship
POPT   = population table
TIME   = actual time during simulation

Labor is one of the primary inputs in the production of non-energy goods and services. Historically, the domestic employed labor force had been approximately 40 percent of the population, as is shown in Table 4.3. Part of this labor force has been employed in the production of energy sources. The energy sector, however, being highly capital-intensive, has historically employed less than 2 percent of the domestic labor force.[5] For this reason, in the ECONOMY1 model it is assumed that the domestic labor force is involved only in the production of nonenergy goods and services.

FIGURE 4.4

The Population Table Function

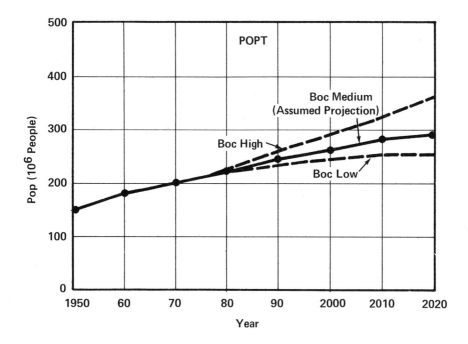

Note: Boc = U.S. Bureau of the Census.
Source: Constructed by the author.

Thus, the normal fraction of population employed in the nonenergy sector is taken to be 0.4. The population in a given year, multiplied by this normal fraction, gives the employed labor force in the non-energy sector.

$$\text{ELF.K} = \text{POP.K*NFPE} \qquad\qquad 2.0\ A$$

$$\text{NFPE} = 0.4 \qquad\qquad 2.1\ C$$

where

      ELF   = employed labor force (people)
      POP   = population (people)
      NFPE = normal fraction of population employed

TABLE 4.3

The Relationship between the Population
and the Labor Force in the United States
(in millions)

Year	Population	Labor Force	Unemployed	Employed Labor Force	Percent of Population Employed
1950	152	64	3.3	60.7	40.0
1955	166	68	2.9	65.1	39.2
1960	181	72	3.9	68.1	38.0
1965	194	77	3.4	73.6	38.0
1970	205	86	4.1	81.9	40.0
1975	214	95	7.8	87.2	40.7

Source: U.S. Bureau of the Census, Statistical Abstracts of the United States (Washington, D.C., 1976), pp. 5, 355.

In ECONOMY1, the labor input to production is measured in man-years rather than the commonly used man-hours. Although historically the man-hour input to production (in terms of the average length of the workweek) has declined slightly for production workers, there are no data available on the workweek duration of managerial and agricultural workers. Thus, there is no reason to suppose that there is a difference between using man-years and man-hours, as measures of labor input. If for some reason a user of the model prefers to use man-hours, the equation for ELF could easily be altered.

The Labor Productivity and Wages Sector

The purpose here is to determine the real wage rate used in computing labor's share of income. Labor's share of income is then used to find capital's share of income within the model as a residual. Moreover, labor's share of income influences the rate of substitution of capital for labor in the model.

Historically, the increases in real wage rate have been closely related to increases in labor productivity. Table 4.4 shows the

TABLE 4.4

Output and Compensation per Man–Year in the United States

	Gross National Product (billions of 1958 dollars)	Employed Labor Force (millions)	GNP per Employee (dollars)	GNP per Employee Index (1950 = 1)	Compensation per Employee (1958 dollars)	Compensation per Employee Index (1950 = 1)
1950	355.3	60.7	5,866	1.000	3,168	1.000
1955	438.0	65.1	6,716	1.145	3,761	1.187
1960	487.7	68.1	7,142	1.218	4,142	1.307
1965	617.8	73.6	8,370	1.427	4,770	1.506
1970	722.6	81.9	8,832	1.506	5,480	1.730

Sources: U.S. Bureau of the Census, Historical Statistics of the United States, Colonial Times to 1970 (Washington, D.C., 1976), pp. 224–35; and U.S. Bureau of the Census, Statistical Abstracts of the United States (Washington, D.C., 1976), p. 355.

FIGURE 4.5

Determinants of the Wage Rate

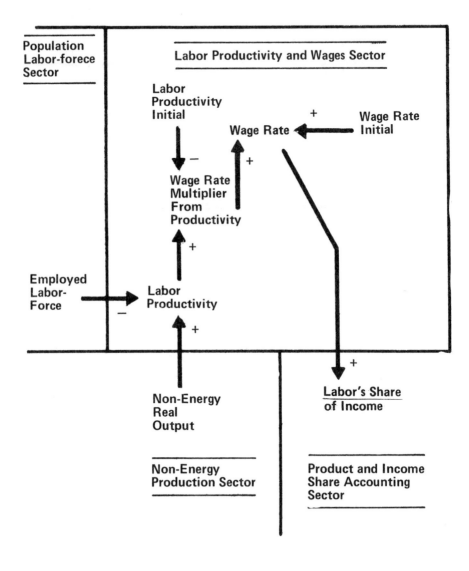

Source: Constructed by the author.

movements in compensation per employee per year and the output (gross national product—GNP) per employee per year. The data indicate that compensation has grown at a slightly faster rate than output per man-year.

On the basis of the historical data, the real wage rate is assumed in the model to be an increasing function of labor productivity. Figure 4.5 indicates the causal factors that influence the wage rate. Labor productivity is measured by the real value of nonenergy output per man-year of labor input, and the value of this productivity, relative to an initial value of labor productivity, determines the wage-rate multiplier in the model. The wage rate in a given year is determined by multiplying the initial wage rate by the wage-rate multiplier from productivity as shown in Figure 4.5.

The functional relationship between the normalized productivity (normalized with respect to the initial value of productivity) and the wage-rate multiplier is derived partly from historical data. For ranges beyond the historical values, the wage-rate multiplier is assumed to have the same relationship as the most recent trends suggest. For example, U.S. Department of Labor estimates indicate that between 1967 and 1975 the real wage rates have grown at the same rate as the growth in productivity.[6] Thus, for ranges beyond the historical values, the wage-rate multiplier is assumed to be linear with a slope of unity as shown in Figure 4.6. In the section on sensitivity analysis, later in this chapter, the sensitivity of the model behavior to changes in the wage-rate multiplier table is tested.

In ECONOMY1, the real wage rate (WR) is determined as the product of the initial wage rate (WRI) and the wage-rate multiplier from productivity (WRMP). The initial wage rate in the year 1950 was found by assuming the nonenergy sector's share of the GNP to be approximately 96 percent.[†] Thus, WRI was found to be roughly $6,000 1975 dollars per man-year.

$$\text{WR.K} = \text{WRI} \cdot \text{WRMP.K} \qquad\qquad 3.0 \text{ A}$$

$$\text{WRI} = 6,000 \qquad\qquad 3.1 \text{ C}$$

where

[†]Historically, the factor share of energy in the GNP has been between 4 and 5 percent.[7]

The computations of initial values of wage rate and labor productivity were made using the data in Table 4.4 and a GNP deflator of 1.87 1975 dollars = one 1958 dollar.

FIGURE 4.6

The Wage-Rate Multiplier from the Productivity Table Function

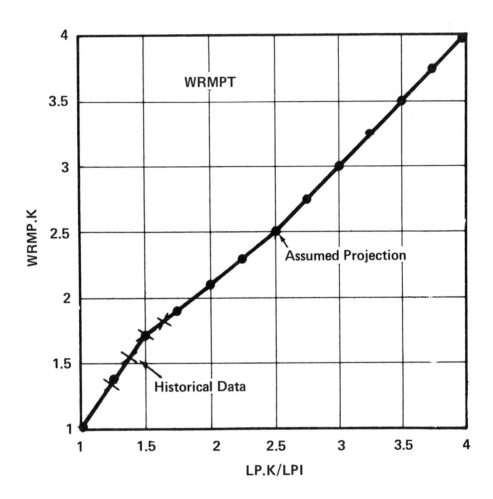

WR   = wage rate (1975 $/man-year)
WRI   = wage rate, initial, 1950 (1975 $/man-year)
WRMP = wage-rate multiplier from productivity
           (dimensionless)

The wage-rate multiplier from productivity (WRMP), as described earlier, is represented as a function of the ratio of labor productivity (LP) to initial labor productivity (LPI). The labor productivity (LP) in the model is measured as the real output of the nonenergy sector, which is the same as the real income of the non-energy sector (NESSI), per employed person per year.† The initial value of labor productivity was found from Table 4.4 in a manner similar to that by which the initial wage rate was computed. The LPI was found to be $10,420 (1975 dollars) per man-year. The DYNAMO equations of this sector are presented below.

$$\text{WRMP.K} = \text{TABHL(WRMPT, (LP.K/LPI), 1, 4, 0.25)} \quad 4.0\ \text{A}$$

$$\text{WRMPT} = 1/1.3/1.7/2.05/2.15/2.3/2.5/2.75/3/3.25/$$
$$3.5/3.75/4 \qquad\qquad 4.1\ \text{T}$$

where

WRMP   = wage-rate multiplier from productivity
             (dimensionless)
TABHL = tabular relationship
WRMPT = wage-rate multiplier table
LP   = labor productivity (1975 $/man-year)
LPI   = labor productivity, initial, 1950
             (1975 $/man-year)

$$\text{LP.K} = \text{NESSI.K/ELF.K} \qquad\qquad 5.0\ \text{A}$$

$$\text{LPI} = 10,420 \qquad\qquad 5.1\ \text{C}$$

where

---

†Since ECONOMY1 is a long-run model, there are no distinctions made in it between product and income. The time constants involved for product to be manifest as income is very small (in the order of few weeks) compared to the time-horizon of ECONOMY1, which is 70 years.

FIGURE 4.7

A Causal Representation of the Nonenergy Production Sector

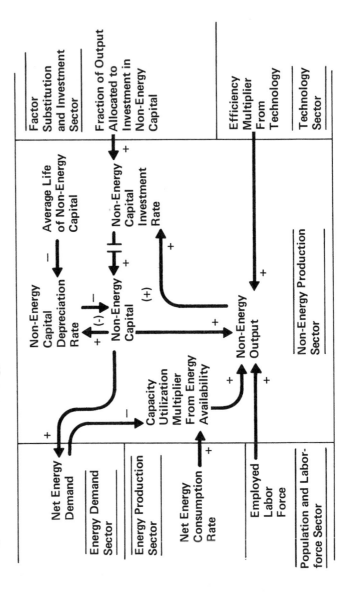

Source: Constructed by the author.

70

LP   = labor productivity (1975 $/man-year)
NESSI = nonenergy sector share of income (1975 $/year)
ELF   = employed labor force (people)
LPI   = labor productivity, initial, 1950 (1975 $/man-year)

The Nonenergy Production Sector

The nonenergy production sector is designed to specify the level of output of nonenergy goods and services for a given set of three factor inputs: nonenergy capital, labor, and energy. Figure 4.7 shows a causal representation of this sector.

Nonenergy capital is a major input in the production process. It accumulates with investment and depreciates over time. In ECONOMY1, nonenergy capital represents the residential, commercial, and industrial capital stock exclusive of the energy capital stock. Capital is represented as a level or a stock variable (NEC), which changes with additions to capital (NECAR) and depreciation (NECDR). The initial value of nonenergy capital for the year 1950 was obtained from data on capital stocks published by the U.S. Department of Commerce.[8] The total domestic capital in 1950 was 543 billion 1958 dollars. This value was converted to 1975 dollars using the GNP deflator of 1.87. The GNP deflator was used for conversion, since a special deflator for capital stocks was not available. Thus, in the year 1950 the total domestic capital amounted to approximately 1,020 billion 1975 dollars. From this value, the energy capital stock value in 1950 was subtracted to obtain the initial value of nonenergy capital. The energy sector capital in 1950 was found to be approximately 70 billion 1975 dollars.[†] Thus, the initial value of nonenergy capital is 950 billion 1975 dollars. The DYNAMO equations representing the capital accumulation process are given below.

$$\text{NEC.K} = \text{NEC.J} + (\text{DT})(\text{NECAR.JK} - \text{NECDR.JK}) \qquad 6\text{:}0\ \text{L}$$

$$\text{NEC} \quad = \text{NECI} \qquad\qquad\qquad\qquad\qquad\qquad\quad 6.1\ \text{N}$$

$$\text{NECI} \quad = 0.95\text{E}12 \qquad\qquad\qquad\qquad\qquad\quad 6.2\text{C}$$

where

NEC   = nonenergy capital stock (1975 $)
DT   = time increment between calculations

[†]The energy capital value was computed from the FOSSIL1 model.

TABLE 4.5

Average Life of Nonenergy Capital

Year	Nonresidential Business Capital (NRBC) (billions of 1958 dollars)	Average Age of NRBC (years)	Residential Capital (NRC) (billions of 1958 dollars)	Average Age of RC (years)	Total Capital (billions of 1958 dollars)	Average Age (Weighted) (Years)
1950	257.0	14.2	285.6	32.1	542.6	23.60
1955	316.9	12.4	350.8	30.0	667.7	21.64
1960	369.6	11.6	419.6	28.7	789.2	20.69
1965	440.8	10.8	482.2	27.7	923.0	19.63
1970	564.3	9.9	544.6	27.6	1,108.9	18.59

Source: U.S. Bureau of the Census, Historical Statistics of the United States, Colonial Times to 1970 (Washington, D.C., 1976), pp. 259-61.

NECAR = nonenergy capital addition rate (1975 $/year)
NECDR = nonenergy capital depreciation rate (1975 $/year)
NECI = nonenergy capital stock, initial (1975 $)

The nonenergy capital depreciation rate (NECDR) is determined in the model by simply dividing the capital by the average lifetime of capital (ALNEC).[†] In Table 4.5, the average-life parameter is derived. A slight declining trend in average life, observed in the table, may be partly due to technological obsolescence during the last two decades of rapid changes in the production processes. Further, it is likely that the data from the Department of Commerce do not reflect the added life of capital goods and of residential structures due to secondary and tertiary exchanges in the market. In ECONOMY1 it was assumed that the average life of capital is approximately 20 years and will not change significantly during the time horizon of the present analysis, that is, until 2020. The DYNAMO equations representing the depreciation rate of capital are presented below.

$$NECDR.KL = NEC.K/ALNEC \qquad\qquad 7.0\ R$$

$$ALNEC \quad = 20 \qquad\qquad 7.1\ C$$

where

NECDR = nonenergy capital depreciation rate (1975 $/year)
NEC   = nonenergy capital stock (1975 $)
ALNEC = average life of nonenergy capital stock (years)

The rate at which additions to nonenergy capital (NECAR) occur is represented as a delayed function of the investment rate (NECIR). Since no data were available for estimating the length of this investment lag, it was assumed to be five years.[‡] A third-order

---

[†]Such an assumption implies that the true economic depreciation of capital is approximated by a declining balance method of depreciation.
[‡]In short-term econometric models of the U.S. economy, the investment lags commonly used range from one to three years. At the higher extreme, the implication is that the total time elapsed between the investment decision and the completion of capital projects is on the average three years. This would imply a time constant of a year and one-half for a third-order material delay, which is too

material delay (DELAY3) with a time constant (NECAD) of five years was used to represent the delay in construction of capital projects. Sensitivity testing on the length of the investment lag, which is shown later, indicates that for substantial perturbations around the value of five years, the model behavior is not significantly altered.

$$\text{NECAR.KL} = \text{DELAY3(NECIR.JK, NECAD)} \qquad \text{8.0 R}$$

$$\text{NECAD} \quad = 5 \qquad\qquad\qquad\qquad \text{8.1 C}$$

where

NECAR = nonenergy capital addition rate (1975 $/year)
DELAY3 = third-order material delay
NECIR = nonenergy capital investment rate (1975 $/year)
NECAD = nonenergy capital addition delay (years)

In ECONOMY1 the nonenergy investment rate is determined within the factor substitution sector. The determinants of the investment rate (NECIR) are presented later, along with the description of the factor substitution process.

The nonenergy output is determined in the model by using a production function that specifies the technical relationship between the factor inputs and the output. The production function is of the following form.

$$Y = A * R * C^{a} * L^{(1-a)} * \text{CUMFEA}$$

where

Y   = the nonenergy output
A   = a constant
R   = the Hick's neutral technical change and is assumed to be a function of cumulative inputs in research and development[10]
C   = the nonenergy capital input
L   = the employed labor force
a   = the production function parameter
CUMFEA = the capacity utilization multiplier from energy availability and is a function of the ratio of net

---

small considering the time-horizon of ECONOMY1. Thus, a five year time constant was chosen. [9]

"energy available for consumption and the net
energy demanded.

Implicit in the form of production function chosen here is the assumption that energy and capital are complementary factors. A given level
of capital, for example, specifies a demand for energy during the
operation of the capital equipment. Over the long run, the relationship between capital and the energy it requires per unit of time may
change due to substitution of more efficient capital goods. This
assumption of complementarity between capital and energy in the
short run, is consistent with the real world. For example, a piece
of machinery such as a lathe requires a certain amount of energy
input to be operated at the rated capacity over a certain duration.
The ratio of the energy input to the product output for the lathe is a
rigid parameter determined by the embodied technology.[†] This
embodied technology is not altered in the short run. If for some
reason, the energy input for operating the lathe is curtailed, then
the utilization of the machine is also correspondingly reduced. This
mechanism is represented in the production function by the availability multiplier CUMFEA.

The model employs a Cobb–Douglas production function with
constant returns to scale from its inputs—nonenergy capital and
labor. Since our concern here is with the long-run disequilibrium
effects, the Cobb–Douglas form satisfies many of the requirements
of a long-run production function, and was chosen largely for ease
of representation.[11] The Cobb–Douglas production function implies
a unit elasticity of substitution between capital and labor. This
means that a 1 percent increase in the wage rate relative to the capital rental rate would cause a 1 percent increase in the capital to
labor ratio.[12] The parameter a in the production function was
assumed to be equal to 0.33.[13] The DYNAMO equation for nonenergy
output is given below.

$$\text{NEOUT.K} = (\text{EMFT.K})((\text{NEC.K})\wedge A)((\text{ELF.K})\wedge$$
$$(1 - A)) * \text{CF.K} * \text{CUMFEA.K} \qquad 9.0\ A$$

$$A \qquad = 0.33 \qquad\qquad 9.1\ C$$

[†]In essence, the derived demand for energy is computed from
a fixed coefficient relationship between nonenergy capital and its
energy use at full capacity of operation during a year. The shift in
this relationship is the energy conservation response shown in the
bottom loop of Figure 4.3.

where

NEOUT = nonenergy output (1975 $/year)
EMFT = efficiency multiplier from technology (dimensionless)
NEC = nonenergy capital stock (1975 $)
A = production function parameter
ELF = employed labor force (people)
CF = conversion factor
CUMFEA = capacity utilization multiplier from energy availability

The conversion factor (CF) in the above equation is the constant term in the production function and it assures the dimensional consistency of the equation. The conversion factor was computed as shown below.

Assume the capacity utilization multiplier from energy availability (CUMFEA) and the efficiency multiplier from technology (EMFT) in 1950 to be equal to one. Then, the nonenergy product in 1950 (NEPI) and the employed labor force in 1950 can be used to compute the conversion factor from the production function relationship. The nonenergy product in 1950 (NEPI) was found to be 600 billion 1975 dollars. The employed labor force and the initial capital in 1950 were, respectively, 61 million people and 950 billion 1975 dollars. The CF was computed within the program using the following equation:

$$CF.K = (NEPI)/(((NECI) \char`^ A)((ELFI) \char`^ (1 - A)))   \qquad 10.0 \text{ A}$$

$$NEPI = 600E9   \qquad 10.1 \text{ C}$$

$$ELFI = 61E6   \qquad 10.2 \text{ C}$$

where

CF = conversion factor
NEPI = nonenergy product, initial, 1950 (1975 $/year)
NECI = nonenergy capital stock, initial (1975 $)
A = production function parameter
ELFI = employed labor force, initial, 1950 (people)

The capacity utilization multiplier from energy availability (CUMFEA) in the production function represents the energy shortage effects in the model. When energy availability is zero, the nonenergy output will also be zero. Similarly, when energy availability equals one, then energy ceases to be a constraining factor in the production function. At these two extremes, the value of CUMFEA is respectively equal to zero and one. In the ECONOMY1 model the variable CUMFEA is represented as a nonlinear function of the ratio of energy available for consumption (NECR) at the end-use level to the net energy demanded (NED). This functional relationship is indicated in Figure 4.8. The nonlinear reference relationship implies that for small degrees of shortages the output will be reduced less than proportionately. For example, a 10 percent shortage in the availability of natural gas can cause serious inconveniences in the form of lower room temperatures and perhaps a few days of work stoppages. Moreover, inventories of alternate fuels, such as diesel oil, propane, or wood, will be substituted during minor shortages. If the shortages are over 50 percent, however, then the effect on the output will be more than proportional. For example, a 50 percent shortage in oil availability could cause serious deterioration of the transportation system and thus lead to multiplicative effects on the national output. A sensitivity analysis using a linear relationship for CUMFEA is described in a later section.

$$\text{CUMFEA.K} = \text{TABHL(CUMFEAT, NECR.K/NED.K,} \atop 0, \ 1, \ 0.2) \qquad \text{11.0 A}$$

$$\text{CUMFEAT} = 0/0.1/0.3/0.7/0.9/1 \qquad \text{11.1 T}$$

where

CUMFEA	= capacity utilization multiplier from energy availability
TABHL	= tabular relationship
CUMFEAT	= capacity utilization multiplier from energy availability table
NECR	= net energy consumption rate (BTU/year)
NED	= net energy demand (BTU/year)

The Cobb-Douglas production function used in determining the nonenergy output may, at the outset, seem too restrictive. In order to test the adequacy of this production function, an alternate form was assumed in the model to test the relative merits of each. The alternate form is the commonly used Constant-Elasticity-of-Substitution (CES) production function.[14] This function is of the form:

$$Y = A * R * (a * C^{-b} + (1 - a) * L^{-b})^{-1/b} * \text{CUMFEA}$$

where Y, A, R, C, L, a, and CUMFEA have the same meaning as

FIGURE 4.8

Capacity Utilization from the Energy Availability Table Function

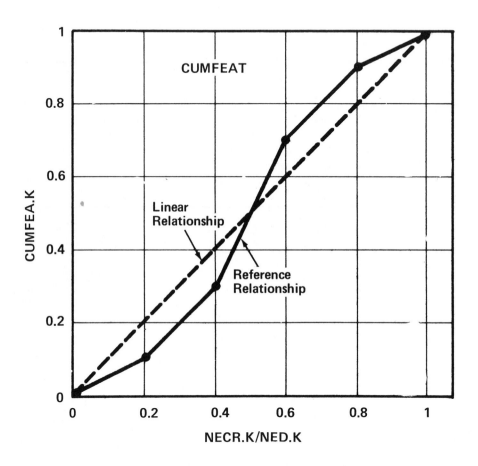

Source: Constructed by the author.

FIGURE 4.9

Test Results with a Constant-Elasticity-of-Substitution Production
Function Using an Elasticity of Substitution, s = 1.25

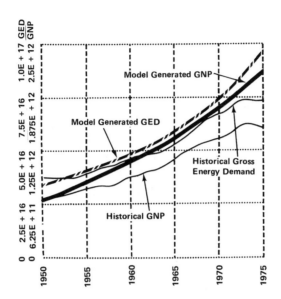

Sources: Historical data on GNP are from U.S. Bureau of the
Census, Statistical Abstracts of the United States (Washington, D.C.,
1976), p. 396; Gross Energy Demand is from Walter G. Dupree and
John S. Corsentino, United States Energy Through the Year 2000,
rev. ed. (Washington, D.C.: U.S. Department of the Interior,
Bureau of Mines, 1976), p. 16. The model-generated data are from
output of ECONOMY1 and FOSSIL1 models.

for the Cobb-Douglas function described earlier. The parameter b,
however, is an additional production function parameter used to
specify the elasticity of capital and labor substitution. The DYNAMO
equations corresponding to the CES production function are as follows:

A NEOUT.K = (EMFT.K)((A * (NEC.K) ^ (-B)
          + (1 - A)((ELF.K) ^ (-B))) ^ (-1/B)) *
          CF.K * CUMFEA.K

FIGURE 4.10

Test Results with a Constant-Elasticity-of-Substitution Production Function, s = 1.15

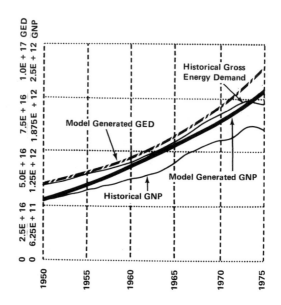

Sources: Historical data on GNP are from U.S. Bureau of the Census, Statistical Abstracts of the United States (Washington, D.C., 1976), p. 396; Gross Energy Demand is from Walter G. Dupree and John S. Corsentino, United States Energy Through the Year 2000, rev. ed. (Washington, D.C.: U.S. Department of the Interior, Bureau of Mines, 1976), p. 16. The model-generated data are from output of ECONOMY1 and FOSSIL1 models.

$$\begin{aligned}
\text{C A} &= 0.33 \\
\text{C B} &= 0.13 \\
\text{A CF.K} &= (\text{NEPI})/((\text{A} * (\text{NECI}) \,\hat{}\, (-\text{B}) + (1 - \text{A})((\text{ELFI}) \,\hat{} \\
&\quad (-\text{B}))) \,\hat{}\, (-1/\text{B}))
\end{aligned}$$

These equations take the place of the original equation no. 9 for NEOUT for the purpose of the present test.

Two possible values of the parameter b were used in testing the CES production function. They are, respectively, -0.13 and

FIGURE 4.11

Test Results with a Cobb–Douglas Production Function, s = 1

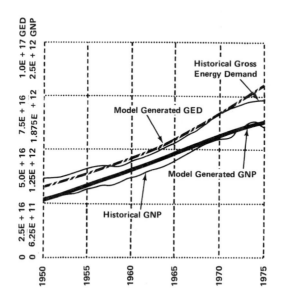

Sources: Historical data on GNP are from U.S. Bureau of the
Census, Statistical Abstracts of the United States (Washington, D.C.,
1976), p. 396; Gross Energy Demand is from Walter G. Dupree and
John S. Corsentino, United States Energy Through the Year 2000,
rev. ed. (Washington, D.C.: U.S. Department of the Interior,
Bureau of Mines, 1976), p. 16. The model–generated data are from
output of ECONOMY1 and FOSSIL1 models.

-0.2.[15] The relationship between b and the elasticity of substitution
is given by[16]

$$s = 1/(1 + b)$$

where s is the elasticity of substitution. Thus, the values of s in
the two test cases are found to be 1.15 and 1.25 for corresponding
b values of -0.13 and -0.2, respectively.

In order to compare the performance of the alternate production function with the Cobb–Douglas function, two criteria variables were chosen. These are the model-generated values of the GNP and the gross energy demand. Figure 4.9 shows the output from the model using the CES function with a b value of -0.2. The model-generated values diverge from the historical data, indicating that the chosen b value may be too low.

A higher value of b was chosen with the same CES function for a second test. Using a b value of -0.13, the ECONOMY1 model was run, the results of which are shown in Figure 4.10. It is seen that despite the change in b value the divergence from historical behavior is reduced only slightly.

Finally, the Cobb–Douglas model was tested (with an implicit b value of zero) and found to be satisfactory in terms of the model output replicating the actual historical behavior. Figure 4.11 shows the test results. Although these tests by no means validate the use of the Cobb-Douglas production function, they at least provide a measure of the usefulness of the function. A recent empirical study reports its estimate of the elasticity of substitution to be close to unity, which supports the assumption of unit elasticity of substitution in ECONOMY1.[17]

The Product and Income Share Accounting Sector

In this sector of ECONOMY1, the basic accounting mechanisms used in computing the real GNP and income to capital and labor are incorporated. Figure 4.12 is a causal representation of the basic accounting scheme.

The GNP in 1975 dollars is computed in the model by adding the real magnitudes of the shares of income of the energy and the nonenergy sectors of the economy.†

$$GNP.K = NESSI.K + ESSI.K \qquad\qquad 12.0 \text{ A}$$

where

---

†Throughout this section the term "share" of income is used in the sense of absolute share. For example, labor's share of income is the same as the sum of all the wages paid to laborers. Further, the term "relative share" is used to denote the ratio of absolute shares.

FIGURE 4.12

A Causal Representation of the Product and Income Share
Accounting Sector

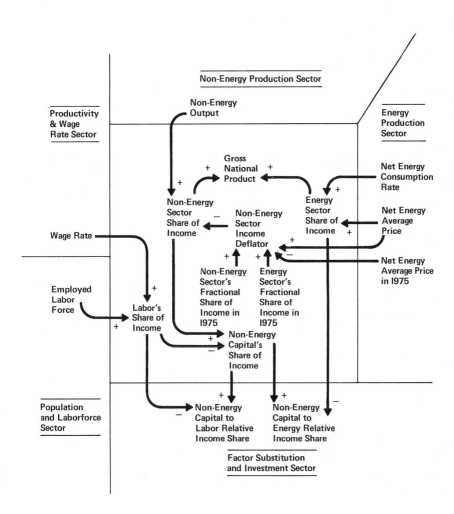

Source: Constructed by the author.

GNP   = gross national product (1975 $/year)
NESSI = nonenergy sector share of income (1975 $/year)
ESSI = energy sector share of income (1975 $/year)

One of the basic assumptions in the ECONOMY1 model is that the real values of imports and exports are equal. Thus, foreign trade balances are not kept track of in the model.

The nonenergy sector's share of income is determined in the model by dividing the nonenergy output (NEOUT) by the nonenergy sector income deflator (NESID). Using the deflator, the current dollar output is converted to constant 1975 dollar income.

$$\text{NESSI.K} = \text{NEOUT.K/NESID.K} \qquad\qquad 13.0\ A$$

where

NESSI = nonenergy sector share of income (1975 $/year)
NEOUT = nonenergy output (1975 $/year)
NESID = nonenergy sector income deflator (dimensionless)

The energy sector's share of income (ESSI) is obtained by multiplying the real price of energy in 1975 dollars and the net energy consumed. The net energy average price (NEAP) is exogenous to ECONOMY1 and is an output of the FOSSIL1 model. NEAP is measured in constant 1975 dollars per Btu of net energy delivered. NEAP also includes a unit Btu tax imposed by government as a policy alternative. Thus, the true share of income to the energy sector must exclude the revenues received by the government from energy taxes (ETAXR), as indicated by the following equation for ESSI.

$$\text{ESSI.K} = \text{NEAP.K} * \text{NECR.K} - \text{ETAXR.K} \qquad\qquad 14.0\ A$$

where

ESSI   = energy sector share of income (1975 $/year)
NEAP = net energy average price (1975 $/Btu)
NECR = net energy consumption rate (Btu/year)
ETAXR = energy tax revenues (1975 $/year)

The value of energy tax revenues (ETAXR) is computed in the model as the sum of receipts from excise taxes on domestic oil and gas, and tariffs on imported oil. The tax scheme is built into the model to allow the effect of a future tax policy to be tested.

$$\text{ETAXR.K} = \text{TOXT.K} * \text{TOPR.K} + \text{TGXT.K} * \text{TGPR.K}$$
$$+ \text{IOTAR.K} * \text{IOCR.K} \qquad\qquad 15.0\text{ A}$$

where

ETAXR = energy tax revenues (1975 \$/year)
TOXT = total oil excise tax (1975 \$/Btu)
TOPR = total oil production rate (Btu/year)
TGXT = total gas excise tax (1975 \$/Btu)
TGPR = total gas production rate (Btu/year)
IOTAR = import oil tariffs (1975 \$/Btu)
IOCR = imported oil consumption rate (Btu/year)

The nonenergy sector income deflator is computed in the model using the Laspeyre formula which provides one possible specification of the deflator index.[18] The index is defined by

$$\sum_{\text{all } i} r_i \cdot w_i$$

where r_i is the price of the i-th factor relative to its price in the base year (1975) and w_i is the share of the gross national income of the i-th factor in the base year. For the present purpose, the deflator could be defined as

$$\text{Deflator}_t = (\text{PNE}_t/\text{PNE}_{1975})(\text{NESSI}_{1975}/\text{GNP}_{1975})$$
$$+ (\text{PE}_t/\text{PE}_{1975})(\text{ESSI}_{1975}/\text{GNP}_{1975})$$

where

PNE   = the price of nonenergy output in the year t
NESSI = the nonenergy sector's share of income
PE_t = the price of energy in the year t
ESSI = the energy sector's share of income

Without a homogeneous nonenergy product, it is difficult to define a unit price for nonenergy output. Hence, it was assumed that throughout the model time horizon the price of nonenergy output is unity. The terms ESSI_{1975}, GNP_{1975}, NESSI_{1975}, and PE_{1975} were computed from historical data.† Thus, the DYNAMO equation for the deflator is specified as shown below.

$$\text{NESID.K} = \text{NFSI75} + (\text{NEAP.K}/\text{NEAP75}) * \text{EFSI75} \qquad 16.0 \text{ A}$$

$$\text{NFSI75} = 0.9 \qquad\qquad\qquad\qquad\qquad\qquad\qquad 16.1 \text{ C}$$

$$\text{EFSI75} = 0.1 \qquad\qquad\qquad\qquad\qquad\qquad\qquad 16.2 \text{ C}$$

$$\text{NEAP75} = 2.5\text{E} - 06 \qquad\qquad\qquad\qquad\qquad\qquad 16.3 \text{ C}$$

where

NESID = nonenergy sector income deflator (dimensionless)
NFSI75 = nonenergy sector fractional share of income, 1975
NEAP = net energy average price (1975 \$/Btu)
NEAP75 = net energy average price, 1975 (1975 \$/Btu)
EFSI75 = energy sector fractional share of income, 1975

The nonenergy sector's share of income (NESSI) is divided between nonenergy capital and labor. Labor's share is the sum of total wages and the government transfer payments. The amount of total wages is computed as the product of the real wage rate and the number of persons employed. Government transfer payments to labor are incorporated in the model to enable the testing of an energy tax policy. It is assumed that the tax revenues accrued from excise taxes on energy and import tariffs are distributed among the non-energy sector capital owners and the wage earners in accordance with their respective shares of the nonenergy sector income. Thus the energy tax revenues (ETAXR) are divided between labor and nonenergy capital by using a weighting scheme. The weights are determined by the original shares of labor and nonenergy capital in their sector income. Such a representation is mainly intended for testing a tax policy that is designed to generate revenues to provide subsidies to industries and households to insulate structures and to promote the use of alternate energy technologies such as solar space and water heating. A user may wish to change the present weighting scheme to test a different tax policy option.

---

†The energy sector's share of the GNP in 1975 was computed by taking the product of net average energy price and the net energy demand in 1975. It was found to be 147 billion 1975 dollars. Thus, approximately 10 percent of the GNP was due to the energy output. [19]

LSI.K = WR.K * ELF.K + GTPL.K   17.0 A

where

    LSI   = labor share of income (1975 $/year)
    WR   = wage rate (1975 $/man-year)
    ELF   = employed labor force (people)
    GTPL = government transfer payment to labor (1975 $/year)

GTPL.K = WR.K * ELF.K * ETAXR.K/NESSI.K   18.0 A

where

    GTPL = government transfer payment to labor (1975 $/year)
    WR   = wage rate (1975 $/man-year)
    ELF   = employed labor force (people)
    ETAXR = energy tax revenues (1975 $/year)
    NESSI = nonenergy sector share of income (1975 $/year)

Nonenergy capital's share of income is determined in the
model as the residual of the nonenergy sector income (NESSI) after
labor's wages are deducted. Capital's share (NECSI) also includes
government transfer payments to capital owners (GTPC). The GTPC
is computed as the residual of energy tax revenues after the deduction
of government transfer payment to labor (GTPL).

NECSI.K = NESSI.K - WR.K * ELF.K + GTPC.K   19.0 A

where

    NECSI = nonenergy capital share of income (1975 $/year)
    NESSI = nonenergy sector share of income (1975 $/year)
    WR   = wage rate (1975 $/man-year)
    ELF   = employed labor force (people)
    GTPC = government transfer payment to capital (1975 $/year)

GTPC.K = ETAXR.K - GTPL.K   20.0 A

where

    GTPC = government transfer payment to capital (1975 $/year)
    ETAXR = energy tax revenues (1975 $/year)
    GTPL = government transfer payment to labor (1975 $/year)

In the present version of ECONOMY1, direct government transfer payment to the energy sector is not represented. It is, however, relatively easy to represent a transfer payment to the energy sector by minor modifications of the equations for ESSI, GTPL, and GTPC.

The Factor Substitution and Investment Sector

The purpose of this sector is to determine the rate at which investments are made in the nonenergy sector of the economy. It is assumed here that the single most dominant factor influencing the investment decision is the profit rate or the rate of return on invested capital in the nonenergy sector. Figure 4.13 shows a causal representation of the investment sector. In this figure, the profit rate is shown to regulate the negative loop governing the capital accumulation in the nonenergy sector. The accumulation of capital, however, is also affected by decisions to substitute capital for labor (automation) and capital for energy (insulation and monitoring devices). Thus the substitution processes tend to make the production system capital-intensive, which in turn has a depressing effect on the profit rate (since the profit rate is defined as profits divided by capital). As the profit rate goes down, the fraction of output invested in nonenergy capital also declines, thus regulating the accumulation of capital.

Investment in nonenergy capital is determined in the model as the product of the fraction of output invested (FOINEC) and the value of nonenergy outout (NEOUT).

$$\text{NECIR.KL} = \text{NEOUT.K} * \text{FOINEC.K} \qquad\qquad 21.0\ \text{R}$$

where

NECIR = nonenergy capital investment rate (1975 \$/year)
NEOUT = nonenergy output (1975 \$/year)
FOINEC = fraction of output invested in nonenergy capital

The fraction of output invested (FOINEC) is expressed as the product of a normal fraction invested (FOINEN) and investment multipliers from labor costs (IMFLC), from energy costs (IMFEC), and from profit rate (IMFPR). On the basis of the historical data shown in Table 4.6, it was found that on the average, approximately 12.5 percent of nonenergy output is allocated to capital formation in the nonenergy sector. Thus the value of FOINEN was assumed to be 0.125.

FIGURE 4.13

A Causal Diagram of the Factor Substitution and Investment Sector

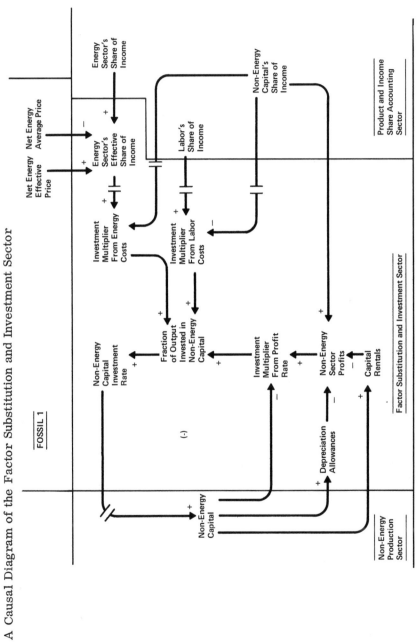

Source: Constructed by the author.

89

TABLE 4.6

Output Invested in Nonenergy Capital
(billions of 1975 dollars)

Year	GNP[a]	Gross Private Domestic Investment[a]	Value of Energy Output[b]	Value of Nonenergy Output[c]	Energy Investment[d]	Nonenergy Investment[e]	Nonenergy Investment to Output Ratio
1950	665	117	42	623	25	92	0.150
1955	816	130	53	763	30	100	0.131
1960	918	132	62	856	26	106	0.124
1965	1,154	188	76	1,078	30	158	0.146
1970	1,357	194	100	1,257	40	154	0.123
1975	1,516	173	143	1,373	43	130	0.095

[a]The constant 1972 dollar GNP and GPDI values were converted to 1975 dollars using the GNP deflator.
[b]Computed by multiplying the net energy consumption and the net average energy price from the FOSSIL1 model.
[c]Computed as the difference between GNP and energy output.
[d]Estimated from FEA data.
[e]The nonenergy investment is the difference between GPDI and the energy investment.

Sources: U.S. Bureau of the Census, Statistical Abstracts of the United States (Washington, D.C., 1976), pp. 394, 433; Walter G. Dupree and John S. Corsentino, United States Energy Through the Year 2000, rev. (Washington, D.C.: U.S. Department of the Interior, Bureau of Mines, 1976), p. 16; Federal Energy Administration, National Energy Outlook, FEA-N-75/713 (Washington, D.C., 1976), p. 295.

$$FOINEC.K = FOINEN * IMFLC.K * IMFPR.K \qquad 22.0\ A$$

$$FOINEC \quad = 0.125 \qquad\qquad\qquad\qquad 22.1\ C$$

where

      FOINEC = fraction of output invested in nonenergy capital
      FOINEN = fraction of output invested in nonenergy capital,
           normal
      IMFLC   = investment multiplier from labor costs
           (dimensionless)
      IMFEC   = investment multiplier from energy costs
           (dimensionless)
      IMFPR   = investment multiplier from profit rate
           (dimensionless)

In ECONOMY1, the factor substitution process is assumed to be influenced by relative factor costs.[†] For example, capital substitution for labor or energy occurs when the income share to nonenergy capital declines relative to income shares to labor and energy. If one can imagine an income statement for the aggregate economy, then from the capital owners' point of view the rise in labor costs would be identical to the rise in the relative income share to labor. In other words, factor costs to firms are incomes to the factors. Thus, the normal response to a rise in the cost of labor would be to substitute capital for labor and thereby conserve on the use of labor. This process, however, is not instantaneous as assumed in the general equilibrium models discussed in Chapter 2. It takes time for capital owners to perceive and react to rising labor costs. In certain industries, long-term contracts with labor do not permit the managers to automate their production processes overnight. Furthermore, there is generally a strong resistance to automation on the part of labor. In ECONOMY1 the relative income shares of capital and labor are smoothed through a first-order information delay with a delay constant of five years in order to represent the time lags involved in the substitution of capital for labor. The length of this delay is an uncertain parameter, and one could debate on the accuracy of using five years. Sensitivity tests on the delay constant (ISSC), however, indicate that even a 40 percent reduction in the

---

[†]See Chapter 3 for a description of the relative income share hypothesis. It is on this hypothesis that the present section is based.

FIGURE 4.14

The Investment Multiplier from the Labor Costs Table Function

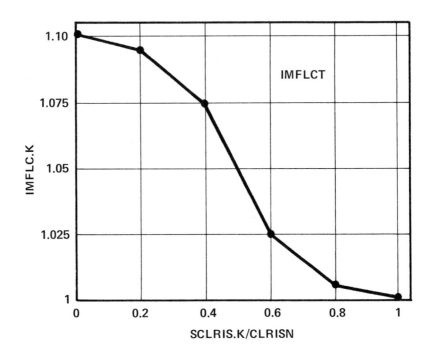

Source: Constructed by the author.

value of the delay constant does not alter the basic model behavior. The sensitivity test is discussed at the end of this chapter.

The investment multiplier from labor costs (IMFLC) is represented in the model as a nonlinear function of the smoothed capital to labor relative income share. The upper limit of IMFLC is taken to be equal to 1.1. This value, for lack of adequate data, is somewhat arbitrarily determined as described below.

From Table 4.6 it is seen that the maximum value of the fraction of output invested in nonenergy capital is 0.15. This value is 1.2 times higher than the normal fraction of 0.125. This factor of 1.2 had to be distributed among the three multipliers IMFLC, IMFEC, and IMFPR. In the model an equal distribution scheme was assumed and thus, an upper limit of roughly 1.1 for each of the three multipliers was computed.† Figure 4.14 shows the assumed nonlinear relationship for IMFLC. The smoothed relative income share of capital to labor is normalized with the initial ratio of income to capital and labor. In 1950, the relation of nonenergy capital income share to that of labor was found to be 0.85. This value was taken to be the normal value of relative shares between capital and labor in the model (CLRISN).‡ The DYNAMO equations for the investment multiplier from labor costs are indicated below.

$$\text{IMFLC.K} = \text{TABHL}(\text{IMFLCT, SCLRIS.K/CLRISN,}$$
$$0, 1, 0.2) \qquad\qquad 23.0\ \text{A}$$

$$\text{IMFLCT} = 1.1/1.095/1.075/1.025/1.005/1 \qquad 23.1\ \text{T}$$

where

IMFLC = investment multiplier from labor costs
      (dimensionless)
TABHL = tabular relationship
IMFLCT = investment multiplier from labor cost table
SCLRIS = smoothed capital to labor relative income share
      (fraction)
CLRISN = capital to labor relative income share, normal
      (fraction)

---

†Historically, the energy costs were stable and hence, energy-induced substitution of capital was not present. Thus, strictly speaking, the factor of 1.2 must be distributed equally between IMFLC and IMFPR only. Such a distribution leads to 1.1 as upper limits of both IMFLC and IMFPR. In the model the upper limit of the energy multiplier IMFEC was also assumed to be equal to 1.1 for lack of adequate data.

‡In 1950 labor's share of income (total compensation) was 336 billion 1975 dollars. The energy sector's share was found by multiplying the net average energy price in 1950 of 1.4 1975 dollars per million Btus and the net energy demand of 30 quadrillion Btus. Non-energy capital's share (the residual from gross national income after deducting energy and labor's shares) was found to be 287 billion 1975 dollars. The GNI (GNP) was found to be 665 billion 1975 dollars.[20]

The initial relative shares of income to capital were used to normalize the relative shares, based on the relative income share hypothesis, which suggests that firms attempt to maintain the initial share, which is assumed to be the desired share. See Chapter 3 for a description of the factor substitution process.

$$\text{SCLRIS.K} = \text{SMOOTH(NECSI.K/LSI.K, ISSC)} \qquad 24.0\ A$$

$$\text{ISSC} \quad = 5 \qquad\qquad\qquad\qquad\qquad\qquad 24.1\ C$$

$$\text{CLRISN} = 0.85 \qquad\qquad\qquad\qquad\qquad 24.2\ C$$

where

SCLRIS = smoothed capital to labor relative income share
(fraction)
SMOOTH = first-order information delay
NECSI   = nonenergy capital share of income (1975 $/year)
LSI   = labor share of income (1975 $/year)
ISSC   = income share smoothing constant (years)
CLRISN = capital to labor relative income share, normal
(fraction)

The nonlinear tabular relationship shown in Figure 4.14 implies that when the relative share of income to capital declines from the normal share by a small amount, the response of substitution through increased investment will be by an amount less than the proportional decline in the income share. For larger declines, however, the substitution response through increased investments will be more than the proportional decline in the relative share. A sensitivity test was performed by changing the upper limit of this function from 1.1 to 1.5. The result, which is reported at the end of this chapter, suggests that the model behavior is not significantly altered. Due to the dominant profit-rate feedback loop, shown in Figure 4.13, the IMFLC table turns out to be not so sensitive. The insensitivity of the model, however, relates only to the upper limit of IMFLC, and it implies that during the model run, the ratio of capital and labor income share in the nonenergy sector does not reach a low extreme, due to the strong influence of the profit-rate variable.

The investment multiplier from energy costs (IMFEC) is represented as a table function in the same fashion as IMFLC, except for the incorporation of a policy alternative. For example, the IMFEC table is designed to test the implication of an accelerated conservation policy, as shown in Figure 4.15. The year in which the conservation policy is assumed to take effect is specified by a variable (ACPYR), which is set to be 2100 during the normal runs of the model. This value can be changed during reruns of the model to a year of user's choice. The DYNAMO equations for IMFEC are presented below.

FIGURE 4.15

The Investment Multiplier from the Energy Costs Table Function

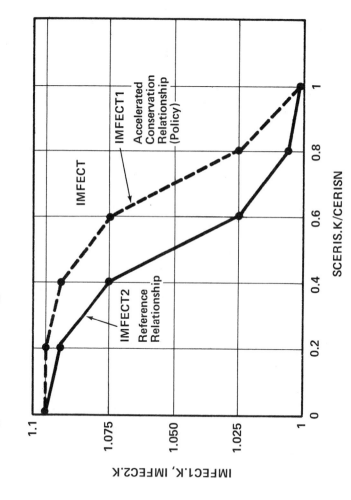

Source: Constructed by the author.

$$\text{IMFEC.K} = \text{CLIP(IMFEC1.K, IMFEC2.K, TIME.K,} \\ \text{ACPYR)} \qquad\qquad 25.0 \text{ A}$$

where

    IMFEC = investment multiplier from energy costs
             (dimensionless)
    CLIP   = function switched during the run
    IMFEC1 = investment multiplier from energy costs 1
             (dimensionless)
    IMFEC2 = investment multiplier from energy costs 2
             (dimensionless)
    TIME   = actual time during simulation
    ACPYR = accelerated conservation policy year (year)

$$\text{IMFEC1.K} = \text{TABHL(IMPECT1, SCERIS.K/CERISN,} \\ 0,\ 1,\ 0.2) \qquad\qquad 26.0 \text{ A}$$

$$\text{IMFECT1} = 1.1/1.1/1.095/1.075/1.025/1 \qquad 26.1 \text{ T}$$

where

    IMFEC1   = investment multiplier from energy costs 1
               (dimensionless)
    TABHL   = tabular relationship
    IMFECT1 = investment multiplier from energy costs table 1
    SCERIS   = smoothed capital to energy relative income share
               (fraction)
    CERISN   = capital to energy relative income share, normal
               (fraction)

$$\text{IMFEC2.K} = \text{TABHL(IMFECT2, SCERIS.K/CERISN,} \\ 0,\ 1,\ 0.2) \qquad\qquad 27.0 \text{ A}$$

$$\text{IMFECT2} = 1.1/1.095/1.075/1.025/1.005/1 \qquad 27.1 \text{ T}$$

$$\text{ACPYR} = 2100 \qquad\qquad 27.2 \text{ C}$$

where

    IMFEC2   = investment multiplier from energy costs 2
               (dimensionless)
    TABHL   = tabular relationship
    IMFECT2 = investment multiplier from energy costs table 2
    SCERIS   = smoothed capital to energy relative income share
               (fraction)

CERISN = capital to energy relative income share, normal (fraction)

ACPYR = accelerated conservation policy year (year)

The smoothed capital to energy relative income share ratio (SCERIS), which influences the investment multiplier from energy costs (IMFEC), reflects two important effects. One is due to energy costs, and the other to energy shortages. In ECONOMY1 it is assumed that at the end-use level decisions to substitute capital or labor for energy are made as a response not only to price of energy, but also to shortages. Shortages cause inconveniences and consumers will try to insulate themselves from the possibility of future occurrences. In order to reflect this aspect of the substitution decision, the actual value of the energy sector's share of income is discounted by a shortage index to give the energy sector's effective share of income. Thus, the effective share is not the actual share of income to the energy sector but it is that share assumed to be perceived by the nonenergy sector in making substitution decisions. When there are no shortages the effective share and the actual share are one and the same.

The shortage index used in arriving at the effective share is part of the output of the FOSSIL1 model. This is denoted by a variable called the net energy effective price (NEEP). The NEEP is obtained by dividing the net average energy price by the magnitude of energy availability (which is one minus the shortage fraction). When shortages are zero, the net energy effective price becomes equal to the net energy average price (NEAP).

The initial value of capital to energy relative income share was computed from historical data, and was found to be approximately 6.8.† The ratio of 6.8 implies that in the year 1950, nonenergy capital's share of income was 6.8 times that of the energy sector.

SCERIS.K = SMOOTH(NECSI.K/ESESI.K, ISSC)   28.0 A

SCERIS = 6.8   28.1 N

CERISN = 6.8   28.2 C

---

†For instance, from earlier computation it was found that the energy sector's share in 1950 was 42 billion 1975 dollars and nonenergy capital's share was 287 billion 1975 dollars. Thus the capital-to-energy relative share was found to be 6.8.

where

SCERIS   = smoothed capital to energy relative income share
                 (fraction)
SMOOTH = first-order information delay
NECSI   = nonenergy capital share of income (1975 \$/year)
ESESI   = energy sector effective share of income
                 (1975 \$/year)
ISSC   = income share smoothing constant (years)
CERISN = capital to energy relative income share, normal
                 (fraction)

$$ESESI.K = ESSI.K * NEEP.K/NEAP.K \qquad\qquad 29.0\ A$$

where

ESESI   = energy sector effective share of income
               (1975 \$/year)
ESSI   = energy sector share of income (1975 \$/year)
NEEP   = net energy effective price (1975 \$/Btu)
NEAP   = net energy average price (1975 \$/Btu)

The investment multiplier from energy costs (IMFEC) was
tested for sensitivity, and it was found that an increase of the upper
limit from 1.1 to 1.5 did not alter the basic behavior of the model.
This suggests that the relative share of income to nonenergy capital
and the energy sector does not reach extreme values during the
model time horizon. In Figure 4.15, the solid line denotes the
normal relationship and the broken line represents the relationship
under an accelerated conservation policy. This policy represents
investment stimulus provided by government subsidies for insulating
structures, solar space and water heating devices, and the use of
passive solar designs.

In ECONOMY1, the mechanism of labor substitution for energy
is not explicitly represented. Since it is assumed that capital and
energy are complementary factors, any reduction in capital intensity
will invariably result in a decline in energy intensity and thereby
implicitly cause labor substitution for energy.

The investment multiplier from the profit rate (IMFPR) is
one of the important behavioral assumptions incorporated in the
model. As profit rate rises above normal, investments in nonenergy
capital increase through the profit rate multiplier. At the other extreme, when the profit rate declines far below normal, investments
decline and eventually reach zero. Thus, when profit rate reaches a
zero level the investment rate likewise reaches zero. The normal

FIGURE 4.16

The Investment Multiplier from the Profit-Rate Table Function

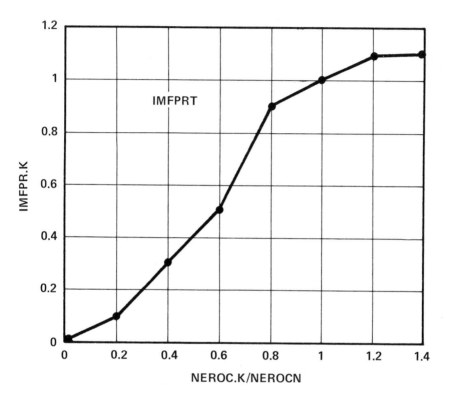

Source: Constructed by the author.

profit rate was found from historical average to be roughly equal to 12 percent.[21]

Figure 4.16 shows the nonlinear relationship between normalized profit rate and the investment multiplier IMFPR. The nonlinear assumption implies that for a relatively small decline from the normal profit rate, investors react less than proportionately in their decisions to invest in capital. For large reductions, however, assuming that alternate investment opportunities are available outside the boundary of the domestic economy, investors will react more than proportionately. The DYNAMO equations for IMFPR are given below.

TABLE 4.7

Capital Rental and Consumption Rates
(billions of 1975 dollars)

Year	Nonenergy Capital[a]	Nonenergy Capital Consumption Allowances[b]	Capital Rentals[c]	Consumption to Capital Ratio	Rentals to Capital Ratio
1950	950	36.9	113	0.046	0.119
1955	1,164	57.3	123	0.050	0.105
1960	1,374	68.6	128	0.050	0.093
1965	1,607	89.3	162	0.056	0.100
1970	1,934	107.6	176	0.056	0.091

[a] Computed as the difference between the total national capital (see Table 4.5) and the energy capital (from FOSSIL1). The GNP deflators were used to deflate capital stock values.

[b] Computed as the difference between the total capital consumption allowances and the energy capital consumption allowances (FOSSIL1).

[c] The sum of net interest, rental income, and proprietor's income.

Source: U.S. Bureau of the Census, Statistical Abstracts of the United States (Washington, D.C., 1976), pp. 397, 398, 433.

$$\text{IMFPR.K} = \text{TABHL(IMFPRT, NEROC.K/NEROCN,}$$
$$0, \ 1.4, \ 0.2) \qquad\qquad 30.0 \ \text{A}$$

$$\text{IMFPRT} = 0/0.1/0.3/0.5/0.9/1/1.1/1.1 \qquad 30.1 \ \text{T}$$

$$\text{NEROCN} = 0.12 \qquad\qquad 30.2 \ \text{C}$$

where

IMFPR   = investment multiplier from profit rate
           (dimensionless)
TABHL   = tabular relationship
IMFPRT = investment multiplier from profit rate table
NEROC   = nonenergy return on capital (fraction/year)
NEROCN = nonenergy return on capital, normal (fraction/year)

Nonenergy return on capital (NEROC) or the profit-rate was computed by dividing the nonenergy profits by the value of nonenergy capital. And the nonenergy profits were taken to be the residual of the nonenergy capital share of income (NECSI) after the deduction of rental charges on capital and the depreciation allowances.[22] From historical data shown in Table 4.7, the average rental rate for nonenergy capital was found to be about 10 percent, and the depreciation allowance was approximately 5 percent of the value of the capital. The rentals were taken to include property rental income, net interest, and proprietor's income. (Rental income is earned by holding an asset whose price is determined at the "beginning of a contract and remains unchanged throughout the life of the contract.")[23] The depreciation allowances or the capital consumption allowances are the value of the capital that firms write off each year for wear and tear.

$$\text{NEROC.K} = \text{NEPRO.K/NEC.K} \qquad\qquad 31.0 \ \text{A}$$

where

NEROC = nonenergy return on capital (fraction/year)
NEPRO = nonenergy sector profits (1975 \$/year)
NEC   = nonenergy capital stock (1975 \$)

$$\text{NEPRO.K} = \text{NECSI.K} - \text{NECC.K} - \text{NECCA.K} \qquad 32.0 \ \text{A}$$

where

NEPRO = nonenergy sector profits (1975 \$/year)
NECSI = nonenergy capital share of income (1975 \$/year)

NECC = nonenergy capital costs (1975 \$/year)
NECCA = nonenergy capital consumption allowances
(1975 \$/year)

$$NECC.K = NEC.K * NECRRN \qquad 33.0 \ A$$

$$NECRRN = 0.1 \qquad 33.1 \ C$$

where

NECC = nonenergy capital costs (1975 \$/year)
NEC = nonenergy capital stock (1975 \$)
NECRRN = nonenergy capital rental rate, normal
(fraction/year)

$$NECCA.K = NEC.K * NECCRN \qquad 34.0 \ A$$

$$NECCRN = 0.05 \qquad 34.1 \ C$$

where

NECCA = nonenergy capital consumption allowances
(1975 \$/year)
NEC = nonenergy capital stock (1975 \$)
NECCRN = nonenergy capital consumption rate, normal
(fraction/year)

In this section three separate nonlinear functions have been presented as parameters that influence the rate at which investments are made in the nonenergy sector. In order to establish confidence in the chosen functional relationships, an attempt was made to estimate the parameters in the multiplicative formulation. Time-series data from 1950 to 1975 were used in estimating the following specification.

$$FOINEC.K = FOINEN * F(SCLRIS.K/CLRISN) *$$
$$G(SCERIS.K/CERISN) * H(NEROC.K/NEROCN)$$

where

FOINEC = fraction of output invested in nonenergy capital
FOINEN = normal fraction invested
SCLRIS = smoothed capital to labor relative income share
CLRISN = normal capital to labor relative share
SCERIS = smoothed capital to energy relative income share

```
CERISN  = normal capital to energy relative share
NEROC   = nonenergy return on capital
NEROCN = normal return on capital
K       = the year
F, G, and H = linear functions
```

A logarithmic transformation of the above equation was used in estimating the coefficients, as indicated below.

$$LOG(FOINEC_t) = a_1 + a_2 \ LOG(SCLRIS_t/CLRISN)$$

$$+ a_3 \ LOG(SCERIS_t/CERISN)$$

$$+ a_4 \ LOG(NEROC_t/NEROCN)$$

From theoretical considerations, the coefficients a_2 and a_3 must have negative signs, and a_4 a positive sign. The regression results, however, indicate that there is a high degree of correlation (0.99) between the two independent variables SCLRIS and SCERIS. With a larger sample size, this problem of multicollinearity could possibly have been avoided, but data restrictions limited this process of estimation. Thus, for the present purpose, the functional relationships assumed for the investment multipliers are taken to be reasonable approximations of reality.

The Energy Demand Sector

In the description of the nonenergy production function it was stated that capital and energy are assumed to be complementary in ECONOMY1. In the energy demand sector the technical relationship between the level of capital and the net energy demanded by the nonenergy sector is determined. The technical quotient is termed the nonenergy capital to energy ratio (NECER). This quotient, when divided into the level of capital, specifies the net energy demand (NED).

$$NED.K = NEC.K/NECER.K \qquad\qquad 35.0 \ A$$

where

```
NED    = net energy demand (Btu/year)
NEC    = nonenergy capital stock (1975 $)
NECER = nonenergy capital to energy ratio (1975 $/Btu/year)
```

FIGURE 4.17

A Causal Diagram of the Energy Demand Sector

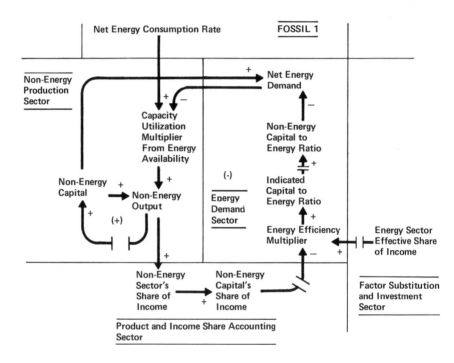

Source: Constructed by the author.

In the last section, the substitution of capital for energy was discussed. As capital is substituted for energy, the technical relationship NECER or the capital to energy ratio must rise, thus reducing the net energy demanded per unit of capital per year. The basic mechanism in ECONOMY1 that causes a rise in the capital to energy ratio is similar to the one that causes a rise in investment multiplier from energy costs (IMFLC). Figure 4.17 shows a causal representation of the energy demand sector. As the capital to energy income ratio falls, due to an increase in net average energy price, the energy efficiency multiplier in the model is caused to rise. This multiplier, in turn, causes the nonenergy capital to energy ratio to rise, after a certain time lag. The negative feedback loop shown in Figure 4.17 is the energy conservation loop through which the demand for energy is reduced as a response to an increase in energy price and to a shortage. Both the price and the shortage effects are incorporated in the smoothed capital to energy income ratio (as described in the last section). The net energy demand causes the capacity utilization multiplier from energy availability (CUMFEA) to go down for a given energy availability (NECR)—which is specified by FOSSIL1: As the capacity utilization declines, the nonenergy output also declines, causing a decline in the nonenergy sector's share of income. The change in the nonenergy sector income influences the gain of the positive feedback growth loop of nonenergy capital, thereby causing a change in the growth rate of output and hence of the GNP. Thus, the net energy availability has a significant effect on the growth process.

The indicated capital to energy ratio (ICER) in Figure 4.17 is used to represent the potential for conservation at any given time. It is suggested that roughly 20 to 25 years must elapse before realizing the full potential of conservation technologies.[24] Thus, a first-order information delay with a delay constant of 10 years is used in the model to represent the lag between the potential conservation possibility and its full realization.

$$\text{NECER.K} = \text{SMOOTH(ICER.K, EESC)} \qquad 36.0 \text{ A}$$

$$\text{EESC} \quad = 10 \qquad 36.1 \text{ C}$$

where

NECER   = nonenergy capital to energy ratio (1975 \$/Btu/year)
SMOOTH = first-order information delay
ICER   = indicated capital to energy ratio (1975 \$/Btu/year)
EESC   = energy efficiency smoothing constant (years)

The indicated capital to energy ratio (ICER) is represented as the product of the energy efficiency multiplier (EEM) and the initial value of the nonenergy capital to energy ratio (NECERI).

$$ICER.K = NECERI.K * EEM.K \qquad\qquad 37.0 \text{ A}$$

where

> ICER = indicated capital to energy ratio (1975 \$/Btu/year)
> NECERI = nonenergy capital to energy ratio, initial, 1950 (1975 \$/Btu/year)
> EEM = energy efficiency multiplier (dimensionless)

The initial value of NECER is taken to be the ratio of the initial value of nonenergy capital (NECI) and the net energy consumed in 1950 (NEDI). In 1950 the nonenergy capital was 0.95 trillion 1975 dollars and the net energy consumption amounted to 30 quadrillion Btus. [†]

$$NECERI.K = NECI/NEDI \qquad\qquad 38.0 \text{ A}$$

$$NEDI \quad = 30E15 \qquad\qquad 38.1 \text{ C}$$

where

> NECERI = nonenergy capital to energy ratio, initial, 1950 (1975 \$/Btu/year)
> NECI = nonenergy capital stock, initial (1975 \$)
> NEDI = net energy demand, initial, 1950 (Btu/year)

The energy efficiency multiplier (EEM) is a function of the smoothed capital to energy relative income share (SCERIS). The initial value of EEM (in 1950) was taken to be unity. The maximum value of EEM is derived from considerations of a hypothetical demand for energy in 1973, if all the conservation technologies were fully utilized. Table 4.8 shows the actual energy consumed in the year 1973 and the hypothetical consumption, assuming that currently known technologies of conservation were in full effect in that year. The actual gross energy consumption in 1973 of 74.74 quadrillion Btus is 1.71 times higher than the hypothetical consumption with

---

[†]These values were derived earlier for the nonenergy production sector.

TABLE 4.8

Actual and Hypothetical Energy Consumption
in the United States, 1973
(quadrillions of Btus)

End-Use Sector	Actual	Hypothetical
Residential	14.07	7.45
Commercial	12.06	7.10
Industrial	29.65	19.22
Transportation	18.96	9.87
Total gross energy consumption	74.74	43.64

Source: Marc H. Ross and Robert H. Williams, "Energy
Efficiency: Our Most Underrated Energy Resource," Bulletin of the
Atomic Scientists 32 (November 1976): 30-38.

conservation. Thus, the upper limit of the energy efficiency multiplier (EEM) was taken to be 1.71. Figure 4.18 shows the nonlinear
assumption for EEM as a function of the normalized capital to energy
relative share of income. In this figure two separate assumptions
are indicated: the reference relationship and an accelerated conservation policy relationship. It is assumed that the accelerated conservation measures do not alter the upper limit of the efficiency multiplier table. However, they do alter the speed of response in
implementing conservation technologies. With increased incentives
such as subsidies for insulation of structures, people tend to
respond at a faster rate in conserving energy than with no incentives.
The upper limit of efficiency is, however, determined by technology,
and subsidies for conservation will not alter this upper limit. Thus,
the accelerated conservation policy merely enables society to reach
this upper limit at a faster rate than otherwise.

The accelerated conservation policy affects not only the efficiency multiplier table in the model, but also the investment multiplier from the energy costs table, as seen in the last section. These
two table functions are designed to capture approximately the syn-
chronous movement of the additions to national capital and its energy
efficiency characteristic, as they occur in response to rising energy
prices. Of course, this effect would be captured more accurately in

FIGURE 4.18

The Energy Efficiency Multiplier Table Function

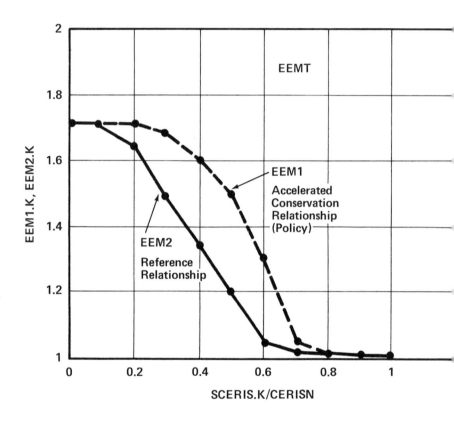

Source: Constructed by the author.

a model where capital of various vintages is separately represented, but for present purposes, the benefits of simplicity in an aggregate model outweigh the gains from a more complex vintage model.

The energy efficiency multiplier (EEM) is used in ECONOMY1 as a substitute for the commonly used price elasticity of demand for energy. The concept of elasticity assumes that the degree to which demand responds to changes in price is independent of the level of price. Over the long term, for example, the demand elasticity itself may vary with higher prices. The nonlinear relationship assumed for the efficiency multiplier makes it possible to incorporate the effect of changing elasticities as a function of price. For example, the flat region toward the right-hand side of the EEM table shown in Figure 4.18 implies that for a small change in relative share of income to capital with respect to energy, a less than proportionate change in efficiency is caused. For larger deviations in relative shares, however, the response is assumed to be more than proportional. Finally, when saturation occurs in potential for conservation, the response of EEM slows down again, due to the effect of diminishing returns. The DYNAMO equations for EEM are given below.

$$\text{EEM.K} = \text{CLIP(EEM1.K, EEM2.K, TIME.K, ACPYR)} \qquad 39.0 \text{ A}$$

where

EEM	= energy efficiency multiplier (dimensionless)
CLIP	= function switched during the run
EEM1	= energy efficiency multiplier 1 (dimensionless)
EEM2	= energy efficiency multiplier 2 (dimensionless)
TIME	= actual time during simulation
ACPYR	= accelerated-conservation policy year

$$\text{EEM1.K} = \text{TABHL(EEMT1, SCERIS.K/CERISN,}$$
$$0, 1, 0.1 \qquad\qquad 40.0 \text{ A}$$

$$\text{EEMT1} = 1.71/1.71/1.71/1.68/1.6/1.5/1.3/1.05/$$
$$1.01/1.0/1.0 \qquad\qquad 40.1 \text{ T}$$

where

EEM1	= energy efficiency multiplier 1 (dimensionless)
TABHL	= tabular relationship
EEMT1	= energy efficiency multiplier table 1
SCERIS	= smoothed capital to energy relative income share (fraction)

CERISN = capital to energy relative income share, normal (fraction)

$$EEM2.K = TABHL(EEMT2, \ SCERIS.K/CERISN,$$
$$0, \ 1, \ 0.1) \hspace{4cm} 41.0 \ A$$

$$EEMT2 \ = 1.71/1.71/1.65/1.5/1.35/1.2/1.05/$$
$$1.02/1.01/1/1 \hspace{3.5cm} 41.1 \ T$$

where

EEM2   energy efficiency multiplier 2 (dimensionless)
TABHL = tabular relationship
EEMT2 = energy efficiency multiplier table 2
SCERIS = smoothed capital to energy relative income share (fraction)
CERISN = capital to energy relative income share, normal (fraction)

The Technology Sector

The purpose of this sector is to determine the efficiency or productivity of nonenergy capital and labor. The efficiency parameter is used in the production function specifying the technical relationship between factor inputs and the nonenergy output. Figure 4.19 is a causal diagram of the technology sector. The causal links shown within the technology sector in this figure are based on the technology hypothesis developed in Chapter 3.

As investments in research and development increase, the level of cumulative inputs also rises after a certain lag. Here cumulative inputs are used as a proxy variable to represent the level of technology used in the production processes. The cumulative inputs in turn determine the value of the efficiency multiplier from technology (EMFT). This variable is used as a multiplier in the nonenergy production function relationship.

One of the primary assumptions used in this sector is that the investment rate in technology is dependent on the same factors as the rate of investment in nonenergy capital. Expenditure on research and development, for example, is viewed by most industries and government as a form of investment and not as a current cost such as wages. A recent study suggests that "there is ample evidence that R & D expenditure decisions are not made in a manner comparable to those involving current costs; rather their treatment is very much analogous to the manner in which fixed-investment decisions are

FIGURE 4.19

A Causal Representation of the Technology Sector

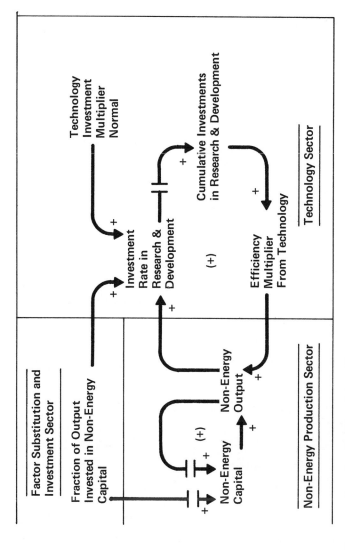

Source: Constructed by the author.

111

TABLE 4.9

Historical Cumulative Research and Development Expenditures
and Factor Productivity Trends in the United States

Year	Research and Development Expenditures[a] (billions of current dollars)	GNP Service Output Deflator[b] (1975 = 100)	R & D Inputs (billions of 1975 dollars)	Cumulative Research Inputs Delayed[c] (billions of 1975 dollars	Total Factor Productivity Index (1950 = 1)
1950	2.87	40.9	7.11	0	1.00
1951	3.36	42.3	7.94	7	1.00
1952	3.75	44.2	8.49	14	1.00
1953	5.21	46.4	11.23	21	1.03
1954	5.74	47.6	12.06	29	1.06
1955	6.28	48.6	12.91	36	1.10
1956	8.48	50.0	16.96	43	1.10
1957	9.91	51.4	19.26	51	1.11
1958	10.87	52.9	20.55	59	1.13
1959	12.54	54.5	23.01	68	1.17
1960	13.73	55.9	24.54	78	1.18
1961	14.55	56.9	25.56	88	1.20
1962	15.66	57.6	27.17	100	1.24
1963	17.37	58.7	29.60	113	1.27
1964	19.22	57.3	33.57	128	1.30
1965	20.44	53.8	38.02	143	1.33
1966	22.26	56.3	39.51	161	1.34
1967	23.61	59.8	39.50	179	—
1968	25.12	61.9	40.55	200	—
1969	26.17	65.0	40.47	212	—
1970	26.55	67.5	39.30	247	—

[a]Including both government and private outlays.

[b]Derived from U.S. Bureau of the Census Data.

[c]Current R&D inputs were smoothed through a third-order material delay with a delay constant of ten years and then accumulated.

Sources: U.S. Bureau of the Census, Historical Statistics of the United States, Colonial Times to 1970 (Washington, D.C., 1976), pp. 197, 965; U.S. Bureau of the Census, Statistical Abstracts of the United States (Washington, D.C., 1976), p. 433; John W. Kendrick, Postwar Productivity Trends in the United States (New York: National Bureau of Economic Research, 1971), pp. 236-37.

made."[25] Thus, in ECONOMY1, the same factors that cause capital substitution for labor and energy are assumed also to influence the decision to invest in research and development. The positive feedback loop shown in Figure 4.19 causes the output to grow with investment in research and development. But the growth process is bounded by the assumption that there is a diminishing rate of return to cumulative investments.

For example, historical evidence indicates that there is a diminishing return in productivity to cumulative investments in research and development. Table 4.9 shows the cumulative expenditures or investment in research and development and the factor productivity index. For lack of adequate data for the years prior to 1950, the level of cumulative expenditures up to 1950 was ignored. Fortunately, this is not a serious problem, since the diminishing returns hypothesis is obeyed regardless of the starting point in time.

The data shown in Table 4.9 include both the expenditures by private firms and by government. This is because government-sponsored research provides a form of subsidy toward the maintenance of many industrial laboratories.[26]

Furthermore, current investment in research and development, shown in Table 4.9, was smoothed through a third-order material delay with a delay constant of 10 years to reflect the lag between investment and the utilization of output from research and development. Historical evidence indicates that the lag between discovery and application ranges from 3 to 50 years, with an average lag of 20 years.[27] This implies a time constant for a third-order material delay of approximately 10 years.

Figure 4.20 shows a plot of the historical relationship between cumulative investments in research and development and the total factor productivity.[28] It is quite clear from the figure that the productivity increases obey the law of diminishing returns. Even if one views the growth rate in factor productivity as a function of time (as is normally done in most macroeconomic models), there seems to be convincing evidence of diminishing returns in productivity over time. This diminishing increase in productivity is incorporated in ECONOMY1 as a nonlinear relationship between the cumulative investments in research and development and the efficiency multiplier from technology. This relationship is one of the important determinants of the long-term behavior of the model system represented by ECONOMY1. The implication of the diminishing growth in productivity is quite serious; for if productivity growth rate reaches zero within the time horizon of concern here, and if the growth rate in population (and hence the labor force) is assumed to be low in the coming decades, then the possibility of a steady-state economy as envisaged by the classical economists is not only highly

FIGURE 4.20

The Historical Relationship between Cumulative Research
and Development Inputs and the Total Factor Productivity

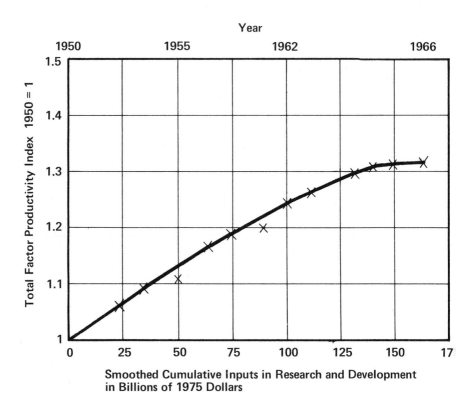

Smoothed Cumulative Inputs in Research and Development
in Billions of 1975 Dollars

Source: Based on data from Table 4.9.

likely but also inevitable. Whether such a low-growth economy could
be sustained, given the present attitudes toward growth, is a different question and is beyond the scope of this study.

In ECONOMY1 the cumulative investments in research and
development (CIRAD) are represented as a level or a stock variable.
Investments in research and development accumulate into the level
after a certain delay. The time constant of the delay between research
start-up and the final application of the output is assumed to be 10
years, as described earlier. Thus, the DYNAMO equations for
CIRAD are,

$$\text{CIRAD.K} = \text{CIRAD.J} + (\text{DT})(\text{RADCR.JK}) \qquad 42.0\ \text{L}$$

$$\text{CIRAD} \quad = 0 \qquad 42.1\ \text{N}$$

where

    CIRAD = cumulative investment in research and development
            (1975 $)
    DT   = time increment between calculations
    RADCR = research and development completion rate
            (1975 $/year)

$$\text{RADCR.KL} = \text{DELAY3(IRRAD.JK, ADRAD)} \qquad 43.0\ \text{R}$$

$$\text{ADRAD} \quad = 10 \qquad 43.1\ \text{C}$$

where

    RADCR = research and development completion rate
             (1975 $/year)
    DELAY3 = third-order material delay
    IRRAD = investment rate in research and development
             (1975 $/year)
    ADRAD = average delay in research and development (years)

The investment rate in research and development is represented in the model as a function of the nonenergy capital investment rate. Further, it is assumed that the magnitude of investments in research and development across the economy bears an approximately linear relationship with the magnitude of investments in capital. For instance, between the years 1950 and 1970, on the average one dollar was spent on research and development for every seven dollars on gross private domestic investment. The average ratio of total R & D expenditures in the economy to the gross private domestic investment for the years 1950-70 comes out to be roughly 0.15. During the sixties, this ratio was higher than in the fifties, due to the space program.[29] Thus, the investment multiplier in technology is taken to be 0.15. The DYNAMO equations for investment in technology are indicated below.

$$\text{IRRAD.KL} = \text{FOINEC.K} * \text{TIMN} * \text{NEOUT.K} \qquad 44.0\ \text{R}$$

$$\text{TIMN} \quad = 0.15 \qquad 44.1\ \text{C}$$

where

FIGURE 4.21

The Efficiency Multiplier from the Technology Table Function

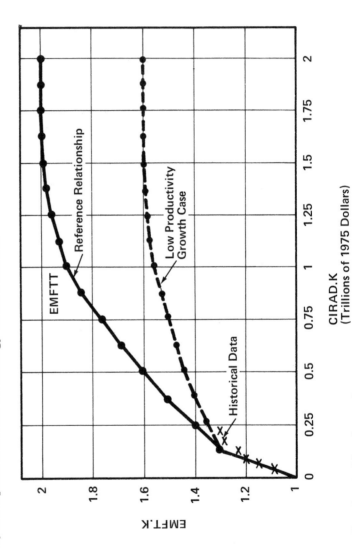

Source: Constructed by the author.

116

IRRAD   = investment rate in research and development
          (1975 $/year)
FOINEC = fraction of output invested in nonenergy capital
TIMN   = technology investment multiplier, normal
          (dimensionless)
NEOUT   = nonenergy output (1975 $/year)

The efficiency multiplier from technology (EMFT) is represented in the model as a tabular relationship. For ranges beyond
the historical values of cumulative research and development expenditures, two possible trajectories of EMFT were assumed. One of
these is based on a smooth extension of the average slope of the
historical relationship shown in Figure 4.20. The second relationship is based on the extension of the most recent trends in productivity growth. These two assumptions are indicated in Figure 4.21.
The reference relationship, the more optimistic of the two, was
used in all the model runs for policy analyses. The low productivity
case, shown in the figure, was used in a sensitivity test, the results
of which are reported later. Any user of the model can incorporate
his own assumptions regarding future growth in productivity by
changing the table function (EMFTT) in the model.
An upper limit of the abscissa in Figure 4.21 of 2 trillion 1975
dollars was chosen, in order to make allowance for cumulative
investments until 2020 (the model time horizon), to remain within
the range of the table. Even with an assumed growth rate of 4 percent per year in cumulative investments over the next fifty years,
the range assumed in the abscissa would not be exceeded in the
model run. This assumption was tested with several different
model runs and the upper limit of 2 trillion dollars was found to be
adequate.

$$EMFT.K = TABHL(EMFTT, CIRAD.K, 0, 2E12, 0.125E12)$$
45.0 A

$$EMFTT = 1/1.3/1.4/1.5/1.6/1.68/1.76/1.84/1.9/$$
$$1.93/1.96/1.98/1.99/2/2/2/2$$
45.1 T

where

EMFT   = efficiency multiplier from technology (dimensionless)
TABHL = tabular relationship
EMFTT = efficiency multiplier from technology table
CIRAD = cumulative investment in research and development
          (1975 $)

THE SUPPLEMENTARY VARIABLES IN ECONOMY1

In addition to the seven major sectors described so far, the ECONOMY1 model consists of a set of 19 supplementary variables. These are used mainly to define a set of output variables that have real-world significance. For example, real income per capita, national income, energy consumption per capita, and gross private domestic investment are some of the variables of interest to policy makers.

The first four supplementary variables in the model determine the labor, nonenergy capital, and energy capital shares of gross national income (GNI). These variables are used in a plot in the next chapter as possible indicators of distributional effects.

$$NECISF.K = NECSI.K/GNP.K \qquad\qquad 46.0\ A$$

where

      NECISF = nonenergy capital income share fraction
      NECSI = nonenergy capital share of income (1975 $/year)
      GNP   = gross national product (1975 $/year)

$$ESISF.K = ESSI.K/GNP.K \qquad\qquad 47.0\ A$$

where

      ESISF = energy sector income share fraction
      ESSI   = energy sector share of income (1975 $/year)
      GNP   = gross national product (1975 $/year)

$$LISF.K = LSI.K/GNP.K \qquad\qquad 48.0\ A$$

where

      LISF   = labor income share fraction
      LSI   = labor share of income (1975 $/year)
      GNP   = gross national product (1975 $/year)

$$TCISF.K = NECISF.K + ESISF.K \qquad\qquad 49.0\ A$$

where

      TCISF = total capital income share fraction
      NECISF = nonenergy capital income share fraction
      ESISF   = energy sector income share fraction

The national income is computed in the model as a supplementary variable. It is defined as equal to the net national product, and is determined by finding the difference between the gross national product and the capital consumption allowances. The capital consumption allowances include depreciation allowances from the nonenergy sector and the noncash charges from each of the four energy production sectors in FOSSIL1.

$$NI.K = GNP.K - TCCA.K \qquad\qquad 50.0\ A$$

where

NI   = national income (1975 \$/year)
GNP = gross national product (1975 \$/year)
TCCA = total capital consumption allowances (1975 \$/year)

$$TCCA.K = NECCA.K + ECCA.K \qquad\qquad 51.0\ A$$

where

TCCA = total capital consumption allowances (1975 \$/year)
NECCA = nonenergy capital consumption allowances
    (1975 \$/year)
ECCA = energy capital consumption allowances
    (1975 \$/year)

$$ECCA.K = DONCC.K + TGNCC.K + SENCC.K + DCNCC.K$$
$$52.0\ A$$

where

ECCA = energy capital consumption allowances
    (1975 \$/year)
DONCC = domestic oil noncash charges (1975 \$/year)
TGNCC = total gas noncash charges (1975 \$/year)
SENCC = steam electric noncash charges (1975 \$/year)
DCNCC = domestic coal noncash charges (1975 \$/year)

The gross private domestic investment is defined as the sum of energy and nonenergy capital investments. The energy sector investments are determined as the sum of investments made by each of the four energy production sectors in FOSSIL1. Two ratios are also defined for use as output variables: gross private domestic investment as a fraction of GNP, and energy investments as a fraction of GNP.

$$GPDI.K = NECIR.JK + EINV.K \qquad\qquad 53.0\ A$$

where

GPDI   = gross private domestic investment (1975 $/year)
NECIR = nonenergy capital investment rate (1975 $/year)
EINV   = energy sector investments (1975 $/year)

$$GPDIGF.K = GPDI.K/GNP.K \qquad\qquad 54.0\ A$$

where

GPDIFG = gross private domestic investment to GNP fraction
GPDI   = gross private domestic investment (1975 $/year)
GNP   = gross national product (1975 $/year)

$$EINVGF.K = EINV.K/GNP.K \qquad\qquad 55.0\ A$$

where

EINVGF = energy investments to GNP fraction
EINV   = energy sector investments (1975 $/year)
GNP   = gross national product (1975 $/year)

$$EINV.K = DOINV.K + TGINV.K + SEINV.K \qquad\qquad 56.0\ A$$

where

EINV   = energy sector investments (1975 $/year)
DOINV = domestic oil investments (1975 $/year)
TGINV = total gas investments (1975 $/year)
DCINV = domestic coal investments (1975 $/year)
SEINV = steam electric investments (1975 $/year)

The total consumption expenditure in the economy is computed in the model as the difference between the gross national product and the gross private domestic investment. Consumption per capita is also determined in the model by dividing consumption expenditure by population.

$$CONS.K = GNP.K - GPDI.K \qquad\qquad 57.0\ A$$

where

CONS   = consumption (1975 $/year)
GNP   = gross national product (1975 $/year)
GPDI   = gross private domestic investment (1975 $/year)

$$CONSPC.K = (GNP.K)/POP.K \qquad \qquad 58.0 \text{ A}$$

where

CONSPC = consumption per capita (1975 $/year/person)
GNP   = gross national product (1975 $/year)
GPDI   = gross private domestic investment (1975 $/year)
POP   = population (people)

The value of energy costs per capita is defined in the model as the energy sector income per member of population. Similarly, the real income per capita is defined as the national income per member of the population. Also, a variable indicating energy cost per capita as a fraction of real income per capita is computed. This variable is used to find the fraction of per capita real income that is spent on energy.

$$ECPC.K = ESSI.K/POP.K \qquad \qquad 59.0 \text{ A}$$

where

ECPC   = energy cost per capita (1975 $/year/person)
ESSI   = energy sector share of income (1975 $/year)
POP   = population (people)

$$RIPC.K = NI.K/POP.K \qquad \qquad 60.0 \text{ A}$$

where

RIPC   = real income per capita (1975 $/year/person)
NI   = national income (1975 $/year)
POP   = population (people)

$$ECPCF.K = ECPC.K/RIPC.K \qquad \qquad 61.0 \text{ A}$$

where

ECPCF = energy costs as a fraction of real income
ECPC   = energy cost per capita (1975 $/year/person)
RIPC   = real income per capita (1975 $/year/person)

Finally, three additional ratios are defined for use later in plotted output. The first is nonenergy profits as a fraction of gross national product. The other two ratios are the per capita net energy consumption rate and the gross national product per capita.

$$\text{NEPFGN.K} = \text{NEPRO.K/GNP.K} \qquad\qquad 62.0\ \text{A}$$

where

NEPFGN = nonenergy profits as a fraction of GNP
NEPRO = nonenergy sector profits (1975 \$/year)
GNP   = gross national product (1975 \$/year)

$$\text{PCNEC.K} = \text{NECR.K/POP.K} \qquad\qquad 63.0\ \text{A}$$

where

PCNEC = per capita net energy consumption
         (Btu/person/year)
NECR   = net energy consumption rate (Btu/year)
POP   = population (people)

$$\text{GNPPC.K} = \text{GNP.K/POP.K} \qquad\qquad 64.0\ \text{A}$$

where

GNPPC = gross national product per capita
         (1975 \$/person/year)
GNP   = gross national product (1975 \$/year)
POP   = population (people)

TESTS OF CONFIDENCE IN THE ECONOMY1 MODEL

In order to establish confidence in the utility of ECONOMY1 to a policy maker, two different tests are shown in this section.[30] The first test compares the model-generated behavior of several important variables with their actual historical behavior, and indicates whether there is a close correspondence between the behavior of the model system and the behavior of the real system. The second test is the parameter sensitivity test, which indicates the sensitivity of the model behavior to changes in uncertain parameter values. Ideally, the model should be insensitive to changes in the values of uncertain parameters. This helps to preserve the basic policy recommendations

FIGURE 4.22

Historical Behavior of Selected Variables from the U.S. Economy

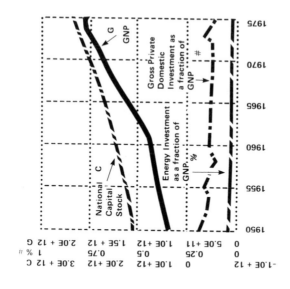

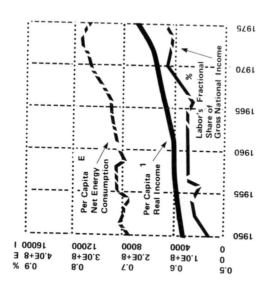

FIGURE 4.22 continued

National Capital: U.S. Bureau of the Census, Historical Statistics of the United States, Colonial Times to 1970 (Washington, D.C., 1976), pp. 259–61; and Statistical Abstracts of the United States, p. 428.

Gross Private Domestic Investment as a Fraction of Gross National Product: Computed from data in Statistical Abstracts of the United States, p. 394; and Historical Statistics of the United States, p. 197.

Energy Investments as a Fraction of GNP: Computed from Federal Energy Administration, National Energy Outlook, FEA-N-75/713 (Washington, D.C.: FEA, 1976), p. 295.

Per Capita Net Energy Consumption: United States Energy Through the Year 2000, rev., p. 16.

Real Income Per Capita: Historical Statistics of the United States, p. 225; and Statistical Abstracts of the United States, p. 396.

Labor's Share of Income: Historical Statistics of the United States, p. 235; and Statistical Abstracts of the United States, p. 397.

FIGURE 4.23

ECONOMY1 Model-Generated Behavior of Selected Variables from the U.S. Economy

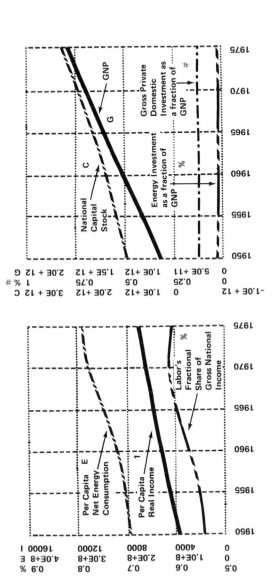

Source: ECONOMY1 model output.

125

that emerge from the use of the model despite the presence of uncertain parameters.

Comparison of the Real and the Model System Behaviors

Figures 4.22 and 4.23 show the real and the model system behaviors of seven key variables. As seen from these two figures, there is a fairly close conformity between the behaviors of the real system and the model system during the historical period (1950-75). This test is also known as the "Mistaken Identity Test," since there is a possibility that an observer might mistake the model system output for historical data.

The Parameter Sensitivity Test

All the parameters in the ECONOMY1 model that could not be satisfactorily estimated for lack of data were changed by 40 to 100 percent from their assumed values for this test. In all, 13 parameters (roughly two-thirds of the model parameters) were tested. Table 4.10 shows the test results. The tabular form for display of results was chosen over plotted outputs simply for convenience. Six output variables were chosen for comparison of their deviations from the reference run values.

The tests indicate that the model is relatively sensitive to assumptions regarding population (which is exogenous to the model), the relationship between labor productivity and the real wage rate (the WRMP table), and the growth rate in factor productivity (the EMFT table). The sensitivity of these three assumptions is to be expected considering their influence on the capital accumulation process (the positive feedback loop in Figure 4.3). The other ten parameters were found to be insensitive in terms of their influence on the behavior of the model.

The two tests described in this section by no means exhaust the number of possibilities of those that could be used in testing the sensitivity of the model behavior. Nevertheless, they aid in gaining a satisfactory level of confidence in the performance of the ECONOMY1 model. In social system models, since one cannot perform controlled experiments, the concept of relative validity is dependent on the model user and his specific purpose. If the structure of the model described throughout this chapter is radically different from the mental conceptions of the observer, then no amount of testing will make the model a valid one. Similarly, if a model user is interested in economic indicators such as inflation rates, interest rates

TABLE 4.10

The Results of Parameter Sensitivity Tests on ECONOMY1

No.	Test	Parameter Change	Model Output 1990						Model Output 2020					
			GNP /1	LISF /2	NECISF /3	ESISF /4	NED /5	GPDI/GNP /6	GNP	LISF	NECISF	ESISF	NED	GPDI/GNP
1	Reference Run	-	2.15	.54	.33	.13	75	.145	2.96	.49	.3	.21	75	.15
2	High Population Growth Rate	T POPT=1.52/ 1.81/2.05/ 2.26/2.58/ 2.87/3.22/ 3.62	2.23	.54	.33	.13	77	.147	3.56	.5	.3	.2	88	.16
3	Low Population Growth Rate	T POPT=1.52/ 1.81/2.05/ 2.2/2.37/ 2.45/2.5/ 2.52	2.10	.54	.33	.13	74	.144	2.56	.49	.31	.2	66	.15
4	Historical Rise in Wage Rate	T WRMPT=1/ 1.7/2.4/3.1/ 3.8/4.5/5.2	2.00	.61	.28	.11	61	.114	2.48	.58	.27	.15	60	.10
5	40 % reduction in non-energy capital addition delay	c NECAD=3	2.18	.54	.32	.14	76	.14	2.98	.5	.3	.2	75	.15
6	Linear Energy Shortage Effect	T CUMFEAT= 0/0.2/0.4/ 0.6/0.8/1	2.03	.56	.32	.12	68	.146	2.47	.53	.29	.18	60	.15

(continued)

TABLE 4.10 continued

No.	Test	Parameter Change	Model Output												
			1990						2020						
			GNP	LISF	NECISF	ESISF	NED	GPDI/GNP	GNP	LISF	NECISF	ESISF	NED	GPDI/GNP
7	40 % increase in upper limit of investment multiplier from labor cost table	T IMPLCT=1.5 /1.45/1.3/ 1.1/1.05/1	2.22	.53	.34	.13	77	.147	3.04	.48	.30	.22	77	.15
8	40 % increase in upper limit of investment multiplier from energy costs table	T IMFECT2= 1.5/1.45/1.3 /1.1/1.05/1	2.21	.53	.33	.14	79	.147	3.13	.48	.30	.22	81	.154
9	100% increase in upper ceiling on investment rate	T IMFLCT= 1.5/1.45/1.3 /1.1/1.05/1 T IMFECT2= 1.5/1.45/1.3 1.1/1.05/1	2.28	.53	.32	.15	80	.15	3.18	.47	.30	.23	84	.140
10	40% reduction in income share smoothing constant	C ISSC=3	2.16	.54	.33	.13	75	.145	2.93	.5	.3	.2	74	.149
11	100% increase in energy efficiency delay constant	C EESC=20	2.14	.54	.32	.14	79	.140	3.00	.48	.3	.22	80	.15

(continued)

TABLE 4.10 continued

No.	Test	Parameter Change	Model Output											
			1990						2020					
			GNP	LIISF	NECISF	ESISF	NED	GPDI/GNP	GNP	LIISF	NECISF	ESISF	NED	GPDI/GNP
12.	100% increase in technology delay constant	C ADRAD=20	2.03	.55	.32	.13	70	.146	2.74	.51	.31	.19	70	.145
13.	Low Productivity growth assumption	T EMFTT=1/ 1.3/1.35/ 1.4/1.44/ 1.47/1.5/ 1.53/1.56/ 1.58/1.59/ 1.595/1.6/ 1.6/1.6/ 1.6/1.6	1.69	.58	.3	.12	56	.113	1.91	.55	.3	.15	52	.112

Notes:

[1] Gross national product in trillions of 1975 dollars.

[2] Labor's share of gross national income (fraction).

[3] Non Energy capital's share of GNI (fraction).

[4] Energy sector's share of GNI (fraction).

[5] Net energy demand in quadrillion Btus.

[6] The ratio of gross private domestic investment to gross national product.

Source: From ECONOMY1 model output.

129

in the money markets, and unemployment rates due to business cycles, he will find ECONOMY1 inappropriate for his purpose. In short, a social system model cannot be tested for absolute validity.

There are very few analysts who do not display a sense of healthy skepticism toward macroeconomic data, which are subject to errors in reporting, processing, and aggregating. For lack of better alternatives, parameters have to be derived partially from macroeconomic data and partially from intuitive reasoning. Thus, in order to aid a potential user, the model is designed with sufficient flexibility to allow the testing of alternate assumptions regarding parameter values in a relatively easy manner.

IMPORTANT DYNAMIC MECHANISMS IN ECONOMY1

The ECONOMY1 model contains two major dynamic adjustment mechanisms that largely govern the behavior of the model system— the capital accumulation and the factor substitution mechanisms. In this section several illustrative runs of the model are shown in order to enhance the user's understanding of the inner workings of the model.

Figure 4.24 shows the determinants of the capital accumulation process in the model. The positive feedback loop that causes the growth in capital stock is influenced by the energy sector in the model (FOSSIL1) through energy availability and price. In addition to the energy sector's influences, the gain of the capital growth loop is also affected by the availability of labor, the total factor productivity (or the efficiency multiplier from technology), and the wage rates. For the present purposes, however, attention will be restricted to the model feedbacks with the energy sector. As described earlier, the energy shortages, defined by the ratio of energy available for consumption and the energy demanded, influence the level of nonenergy output through the capacity utilization multiplier. Likewise, energy price influences the nonenergy sector real income through the deflator mechanism.

Figure 4.25 indicates the determinants of the factor substitution process. The negative feedback loop tries to maintain the relative share of income to capital at a desired level by substituting capital for labor and energy. As previously described in the factor substitution sector, the relative share of income reflects both the shortage and the price effects.

The price effect is captured in the model through a deflator mechanism. For example, a rise in energy price causes the deflator to increase and thus, the real value of output from the nonenergy sector declines. Further, labor's share of income in the nonenergy

FIGURE 4.24

Determinants of Capital Accumulation in ECONOMY1

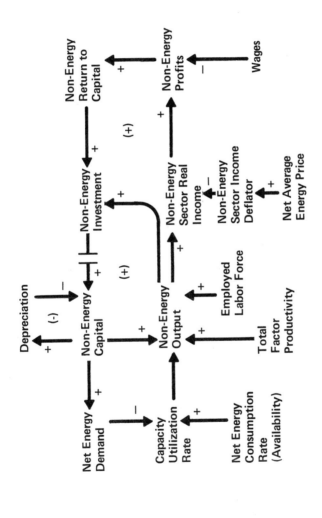

Source: Constructed by the author.

FIGURE 4.25

Determinants of Factor Substitution in ECONOMY1

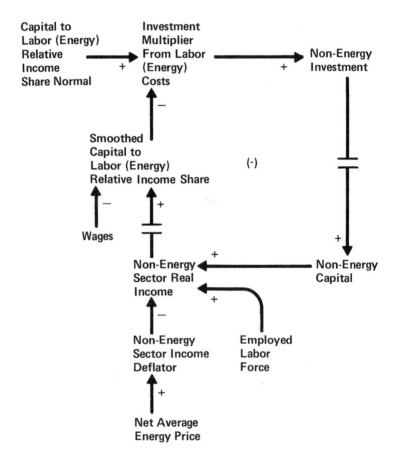

sector is fixed for a given wage rate and the level of labor-force employment. Thus, when labor's share is deducted from the non-energy sector income, the share to capital in the nonenergy sector declines with an increase in energy price.

The shortage effect is reflected through the use of the net energy effective price. For instance, when shortages occur, the actual share of income to the energy sector is inflated by a factor that corresponds to the magnitude of the shortage. This inflated value of income to the energy sector is used simply as proxy information to capture the effect on the nonenergy sector investment decision as a response to energy shortage. Thus, the effective share of income to the energy sector superimposes the shortage information that is due purely to the rise in energy price. This superimposition allows the representation of the effects of shortages on investment decisions through the normal price mechanism.

To illustrate the functioning of these two mechanisms in the model, three different scenarios were simulated. The first, the reference run shown in Figures 4.26 and 4.27, indicates the most likely behavior of the aggregate economy, if no new policies concerning energy are implemented. Due to price and shortage effects, the growth in capital stock is seen to depart radically from its historical growth pattern. This clearly indicates that the energy sector significantly influences the growth in capital stock, and hence, the output in the nonenergy sector.

In the second scenario, in order to see how much of the decline in the growth rate of capital could be attributed to energy shortages alone, the shortage effects in the model were deleted. The changes in the DYNAMO equations that were required to do this are

$$T \text{ CUMFEAT} = 1/1/1/1/1/1$$

and

$$A \text{ NEEP.K} = \text{NEAP.K}$$

These changes were introduced in the model to take effect only after 1975, so that the historical behavior modes would be retained. The output from this model run is shown in Figures 4.28 and 4.29. In this scenario, even though shortages occur in the energy sector, they have no influence on the economy. The basic behavior modes are essentially the same in this case as in the previous case, except that nonenergy capital grows smoothly after the year 2000.

The third scenario involves decoupling the energy sector completely from the rest of the economy by excluding both the shortage and the price effects. In this case the net average energy price (NEAP)

FIGURE 4.26

Reference Behavior of ECONOMY1 Showing Growth in Nonenergy Capital

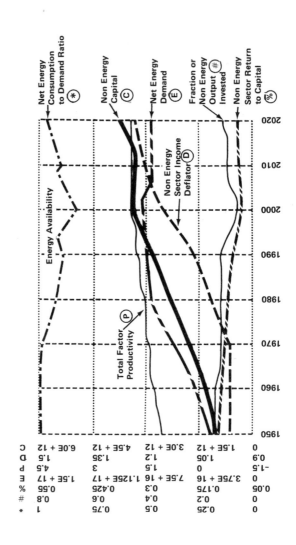

Source: ECONOMY1 model output.

134

FIGURE 4.27

Reference Behavior of ECONOMY1 Indicating Substitution of Nonenergy Capital

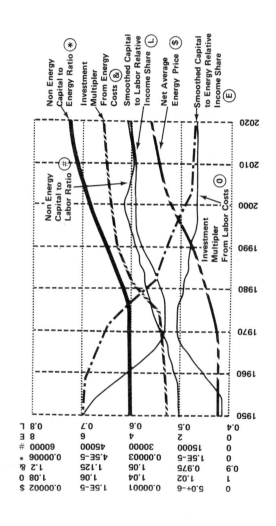

Source: ECONOMY1 model output.

135

FIGURE 4.28

Model Run Showing the Capital Growth Process without the Energy Shortage Effects

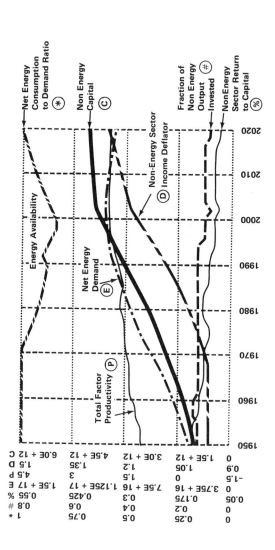

Source: ECONOMY1 model output.

FIGURE 4.29

Model Run Showing the Substitution Process without the Energy Shortage Effects

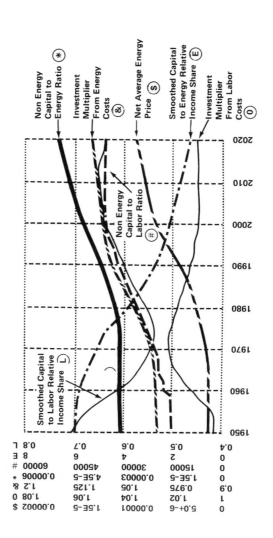

Source: ECONOMY1 model output.

137

FIGURE 4.30

Model Run Showing the Capital Growth Behavior without the Energy Price and Shortage Effects

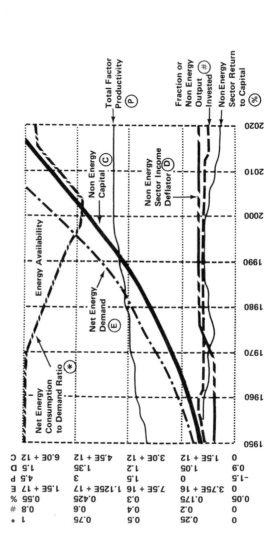

Source: ECONOMY1 model output.

138

FIGURE 4.31

Model Run Showing the Substitution Process without the Energy Price and Shortage Effects

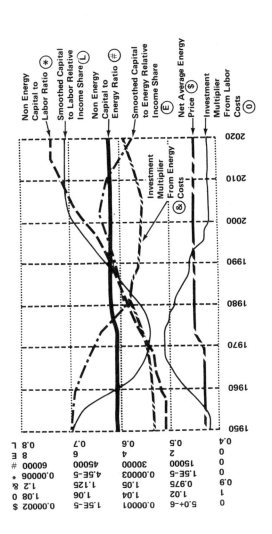

Source: ECONOMY1 model output.

was set equal to its 1975 value of $2.50 per million Btus after the year 1975 in the model. Figures 4.30 and 4.31 show the results from the model run. As one would expect, the nonenergy capital grows at a historical rate of approximately 3 percent per year, and capital substitution for energy does not take place, as indicated by the stable nonenergy capital to energy ratio in the figure. The net energy demand continues to grow exponentially at the historical rate. This case suggests that the price effect in the model is the dominant mechanism influencing the growth of capital.

The two hypothetical scenarios shown in this section clarify the two basic mechanisms through which the energy sector influences the rest of the economy, as these interactions are represented in ECONOMY1.

Finally, it must be emphasized that the ECONOMY1 model is not designed to predict the precise values of macroeconomic variables. Predictions of GNP or energy demand 50 years in the future would at best be meaningless. Thus, the model is mainly intended to project a set of conditional and imprecise behavior modes of macroeconomic variables into the future. For example, the behavior mode that represents the growth in the nonenergy capital stock in the reference run clearly indicates a potential problem. The problem is the very low growth in capital and hence, in output in the nonenergy sector. This is a problem if it is desirable to have continued growth in these variables. Thus, the task of policy designing involves shaping the problem behavior to a desirable one by means of appropriate policies. This is the subject of the next chapter, where the ECONOMY1 model is used to test alternate energy policy options for their relative effectiveness in solving the domestic energy transition problem.

NOTES

1. The FOSSIL1 model was developed by the Dartmouth System Dynamics Group for the Fossil Energy Division of the Energy Research and Development Administration (now the Department of Energy), under contract number E(49-18)-2230. For a detailed description of the FOSSIL1 model, see "FOSSIL1 Documentation"; "FOSSIL1: A Policy Analysis Model of the United States Energy System"; and "FOSSIL1 Technical Appendices"—prepared by the Dartmouth System Dynamics Group, Thayer School of Engineering, Dartmouth College, Hanover, New Hampshire, April 1977.

2. For a detailed description, see Jay W. Forrester, Industrial Dynamics (Cambridge, Mass.: MIT Press, 1961); and Alexander L. Pugh, DYNAMO II User's Manual, 4th ed. (Cambridge, Mass.: MIT Press, 1973).

3. For a detailed description of individual policies in Table 4.1, see Dartmouth System Dynamics Group, "FOSSIL1 Technical Appendices."

4. For a detailed discussion of conventions used in this diagram, see Forrester, Industrial Dynamics, pp. 81-84.

5. See Federal Energy Administration, Project Independence Blueprint (Washington, D.C.: 1974), p. 295.

6. See, for example, U.S. Department of Labor, Bureau of Labor Statistics, Productivity and the Economy, Bulletin No. 1926 (Washington, D.C., 1977), p. 51.

7. See, for instance, William W. Hogan and Alan S. Manne, "Energy-Economy Interactions: The Fable of the Elephant and the Rabbit?" Energy Modeling Forum working paper, Stanford University, Stanford, California, July 1976, p. 2.

8. The net stocks from the U.S. Department of Commerce data on capital stocks were used in initializing capital stock value. See U.S. Bureau of the Census, Historical Statistics of the United States, Colonial Times to 1970 (Washington, D.C., 1976), pp. 259-61.

9. For examples of investment lags, see M. K. Evans, Macroeconomic Activity, Theory, Forecasting, and Control (New York: Harper and Row, 1969), p. 501.

10. See the productivity hypothesis presented in Chapter 2. The parameter R is described in detail in the technology sector. Here Hick's neutral technical change implies a lack of bias in assigning the technical progress to any one factor. See, for example, R. G. D. Allen, Macro-Economic Theory—A Mathematical Treatment (New York: Macmillan, 1968), p. 239.

11. See, for example, Kazuo Sato, Production Functions and Aggregation (Amsterdam: North-Holland Publishing Co., 1975), p. 293.

12. Such an interpretation of the elasticity of substitution is based on perfect competition and profit maximization assumptions. See Allen, Macro-Economic Theory, p. 50.

13. Sources: Murray Brown, ed., The Theory and Empirical Analysis of Production (New York: National Bureau of Economic Research, 1967), p. 18; and Evans, Macroeconomic Activity, p. 501.

14. For a description of the BES production function, see K. J. Arrow, H. B. Chenery, B. S. Minhas, and R. M. Solow, "Capital-Labor Substitution and Economic Efficiency," Review of Economics and Statistics 43 (August 1961): 225-50.

15. These two test values of b were chosen from Ernst Berndt's estimates, given in Ernst R. Berndt, "Reconciling Alternative Estimates of the Elasticity of Substitution," Review of Economics and Statistics 57 (August 1975): 259-68.

16. See Allen, Macro-Economic Theory, p. 53.

17. Berndt reports that the ordinary least-squares time-series estimates "of s approach unity as better methods of data measurement are used." See Berndt, "Reconciling Alternative Estimates of the Elasticity of Substitution," p. 65.

18. Considering the complexity of specifying a deflator index, only a crude measure could be devised for the present purpose. The Laspeyre index serves the purpose adequately. See, for example, Kali S. Bannerjee, Cost of Living Index Numbers (New York: Marcel Dekker, 1975), for a description of various approaches to index number design.

19. For energy demand data, see U.S. Bureau of the Census, Statistical Abstracts of the United States (Washington, D.C., 1976), p. 548. The energy price estimates are from FOSSIL1. The GNP data were taken from Statistical Abstracts, 1976, p. 393.

20. U.S. Bureau of the Census, Statistical Abstracts, 1976, pp. 397-98.

21. The normal profit rate was found from the average of return on net worth data compiled by the First National City Bank. See First National City Bank Profits Tabulations, Historical Summary, 1925-74, New York, 1975.

22. See Evans, Macroeconomic Activity, p. 274, for an explanation of the definition of profits. The present scheme is consistent with the accounting scheme used by the U.S. Department of Commerce.

23. Evans, Macroeconomic Activity, p. 283.

24. Marc H. Ross and Robert H. Williams, "Energy Efficiency: Our Most Underrated Energy Resource," Bulletin of the Atomic Scientists 32 (November 1976): 30-38; and Ford Foundation, A Time to Choose (Cambridge, Mass.: Ballinger, 1974), p. 4.

25. Daniel Hamberg, Essays on Economics of Research and Development (New York: Random House, 1966), p. 127.

26. Ibid., p. 124.

27. For a more detailed treatment of the lag between discovery and application, see Maurice Goldsmith, ed., Technological Innovation and the Economy (London: Wiley-Interscience, 1970), p. 264; and Nathan Rosenberg, Perspectives on Technology (Cambridge: Cambridge University Press, 1976), p. 68.

28. The total factor productivity as measured by Kendrick is used in estimating the efficiency parameter in ECONOMY1. Kendrick's measure allows a fairly consistent estimation of the EMFT parameter, since the assumed form of aggregate production function in ECONOMY1 is the Cobb-Douglas type with a Hick's neutral technical change. See John W. Kendrick, Postwar Productivity Trends in the United States, 1948-1969 (New York: National Bureau

of Economic Research, 1973), p. 14, for a description of the factor productivity concept.

29. See U.S. Bureau of the Census, Statistical Abstracts, 1976, p. 394, for data on research and development expenditures.

30. See Jay W. Forrester, Confidence in Models of Social Behavior with Emphasis on System Dynamics Models, MIT System Dynamics Group Memo No. D-1967, Massachusetts Institute of Technology, Cambridge, Massachusetts, 1973.

5

POLICY ANALYSIS
AND CONCLUSIONS

INTRODUCTION

In this chapter the ECONOMY1 and the FOSSIL1 models are used to analyze a selected set of energy policies and their impacts on economic growth, energy imports, and shortages. In addition, a preliminary analysis of the impact of rising energy costs on low and middle income groups is presented.

Since the models developed and used here are meant for generating conditional, imprecise projections of the behavior of the energy-economy system interactions, it is useful to reiterate the basic assumptions incorporated in the ECONOMY1 model.[†] With the assumptions explicitly stated, the model user is better equipped to judge and interpret the results presented in this chapter. There are five basic assumptions that govern the behavior of the ECONOMY1 model:

The energy sector affects the rest of the economy through shortages and/or income transfers from rising energy prices.

Capital investment in the economy is primarily governed by the realized returns on capital. The secondary causes that influence

---

[†]The results presented later in this chapter should not be interpreted as point predictions of variables such as GNP and energy demand, but as projections of the behavior of the U.S. economy-energy system

The assumptions incorporated within the FOSSIL1 model are not listed here.[1]

the investment rate are the pressures for substitution of capital for labor and energy as a response to rising costs of the latter two factors.

Substitution of capital for labor and energy is governed by the goal of firms to retain the relative share of income to capital at a desired level.

Capital and energy are complementary factors and the relationship between capital used per year and the energy required to operate the capital is rigid in the short run and changes slowly over time as a response to rising energy prices.

The increase in total factor productivity obeys the law of diminishing returns to cumulative investments in research and development.

ENERGY POLICIES FOR TESTING AND ANALYSIS

Although all the policies listed in Table 4.1 in the last chapter could be tested using the ECONOMY 1 and FOSSIL1 models, only a selected few are tested in this section.[2] The selection is made to illuminate important aspects of current energy policy debates in the country rather than to test, in a methodical fashion, the merits and demerits of individual policy options.

Much of the current debate on energy policy in Congress and elsewhere in this country can be classified in three major categories according to viewpoint. The consumerist viewpoint focusses primarily on the price of energy. For example, a scenario could be conceived that would be considered ideal by the consumerists—one in which energy users pay as low a price as possible for as long a duration as is allowed by resource limits. The energy industry viewpoint concentrates on price as a mechanism for inducing investments in domestic energy production, and hence favors a free energy market. The ecological viewpoint focusses on conservation as the primary alternative. This viewpoint is shared partially by both consumers and producers. Even though these three viewpoints are not necessarily mutually exclusive, in this section they are assumed to be so, for the sake of convenience. Four scenarios are developed to represent and compare these three major points of view against a reference case that represents a continuation of the status quo.

The first scenario represents the reference case and is called the "business-as-usual" scenario, in which no new energy policies are implemented. This scenario essentially portrays the evolution of the present system with the continuation of existing regulations on energy production.

The second scenario is termed the "low-price" scenario, which represents what would be generally considered ideal by consumer groups. It is based on an assumption of altruism on the part of the OPEC countries, which use a pricing strategy that maintains the current level of oil prices into the future. In this scenario it is assumed that domestic consumers pay a relatively low price for energy primarily due to the good graces of the oil-exporting countries, and furthermore that no other changes are implemented in domestic energy policies.

In contrast with the low-price scenario, the reference or the business-as-usual scenario assumes that the OPEC oil-pricing strategy, which is the major determinant of the domestic energy price, is to maintain OPEC's export price equal to the marginal cost of oil production in the United States.

In the low-price scenario, OPEC does not maintain a stable price level indefinitely into the future. Instead, it is assumed that it maintains a stable price until its marginal cost of oil production exceeds the price.† At this point, OPEC would switch to a pricing policy based on its marginal cost of oil production.

The third case is the "high-price" scenario, which is composed of three major energy policies that are generally considered to be ideal by the energy industries in the United States. The first of these is deregulation of natural gas prices. It is assumed that the deregulation is implemented starting in 1978, in phases over a five-year period. At the end of the last phase in 1983, the price of natural gas is assumed to be determined by the free market forces of supply and demand. The second policy, similar to the first one, is deregulation of domestic oil prices beginning in 1980. This policy is also assumed to be implemented in phases over a five-year period, ending in 1985. The third policy is imposition of a tariff on imported oil in order to protect domestic suppliers from the vagaries of OPEC pricing policies. It is assumed that a tariff of $9 (1975 dollars) per barrel is to be imposed on imported oil, beginning in 1980.

The fourth scenario, representing the ecological viewpoint, is termed the "accelerated-conservation" scenario. In this case, the government plays an active role in promoting, through the use of tax incentives, conservation measures such as insulation of residential and commercial structures, waste-heat utilization by industries, and energy-efficient transportation technologies. The scenario con-

---

†In the FOSSIL1 model, the OPEC oil reserves and production costs are represented endogenously. Thus, the depletion of world oil resources is captured in the model.

TABLE 5.1

Summary of Test Scenarios and Associated Policies

Scenario	Policies	Effects	Parameter Changes[a]
Business as usual	—	—	—
Low price	Low OPEC[b] pricing policy	OPEC maintains oil price at $13 (1975$) per barrel after 1977. Eventually when the marginal production cost of OPEC oil exceeds this price due to depletion they switch to marginal cost pricing policy.	C OOPS=1 (in FOSSIL1)
High price	Tariff[c] on oil imports	A $9 (1975$) per barrel tariff is imposed on imported oil beginning in 1980.	C IOTARY=1980 (in FOSSIL1)
	Phased oil deregulation	Domestic oil prices are gradually deregulated over a period of five years, from 1980 to 1985. After 1985 domestic oil prices are determined by the free market.	C DODYI =1980 C DODYC=1985 (in FOSSIL1)
	Phased gas deregulation	Domestic gas prices are gradually deregulated over a period of five years, from 1978 to 1983. After 1985 domestic gas prices are determined by the free market.	C TGDYI =1978 C TGDYC=1983 (in FOSSIL1)

(continued)

147

TABLE 5.1 continued

Scenario	Policies	Effects	Parameter Changes[a]
Accelerated conservation	Tariff on oil imports	–same as in high-price scenario–	C IOTARY=1980 (in FOSSIL1)
	Oil excise tax	A $3 (1975$) per barrel tax on oil is imposed starting in 1980.	C TOXTY=1980 (in FOSSIL1)
	Gas excise tax	A $0.50 (1975$) per million cubic feet tax on gas is imposed started in 1980.	C TGXTY=1980 (in FOSSIL1)
	Conservation technologies implemented through general government tax incentives	Energy users conserve by investing in efficiency improvement technologies in response to general government incentives beginning in 1980.	C ACPYR=1980 (in ECONOMY1)

[a]For definitions of the parameters indicated in this table see Appendix D for ECONOMY1 parameters and Appendix E for FOSSIL1 parameters.

[b]In all scenarios except the low price one it is assumed that the OPEC oil pricing strategy is based on the marginal costs of oil production in the United States.

[c]All the tax revenues obtained from tariffs and excise taxes are assumed to be distributed among nonenergy sector capital owners and laborers.

Source: Compiled by the author.

148

sists of three major tax policies designed to discourage energy consumption: an excise tax on oil, an excise tax on gas, and a tariff on oil imports. It is assumed that the revenues from these taxes are passed on to consumers and industries in the nonenergy sector of the economy in order to subsidize the implementation of conservation technologies. This subsidy program is represented as a separate policy in the ECONOMY1 model. †

Thus, there are four policies in the accelerated-conservation scenario, all assumed to be implemented in 1980. The excise tax assumptions are, respectively, 50 cents (1975 dollars) per million cubic feet of gas and $3.00 (1975 dollars) per barrel of oil.

Table 5.1 summarizes the four scenarios and the associated policy alternatives. The scenarios described so far are intended to be only a set of rough approximations representing the four viewpoints—those of the status quo, the consumerists, the energy industry, and the ecologists.

To compare the relative effects of the alternative scenarios on future economic growth and distribution of income, a set of criteria variables—including the gross national product, oil imports, energy shortages, and real income per capita—are chosen for output plots. First, the issue of the energy sector influence on economic growth is considered. Later, the equity issue is discussed in detail.

ENERGY AND ECONOMIC GROWTH

Figures 5.1 and 5.2 show the behavior modes of the U.S. energy system and the economy in the business-as-usual scenario. Based on ECONOMY1 and FOSSIL1 models, these behavior modes specify the most likely course of the U.S. energy-economy system, if no new policy changes are implemented.

The growth in gross energy demand slows down due to price-induced substitution effects in the short run, and due to the feedback from the economy in terms of reduced output in the long run. Imports as well as energy shortages persist throughout the time horizon. By the year 2000 the price of energy rises by a factor of three from its 1975 level and causes the income transfer rate to the energy sector to rise, which in turn slows down economic growth due to its adverse influence on the capital accumulation process. The energy sector's

---

†For a description of this policy representation, see the accounting, investment, and energy demand sector elaborations in Chapter 4.

FIGURE 5.1

Business–as–Usual Reference Projection of the Behavior of the U.S. Energy System

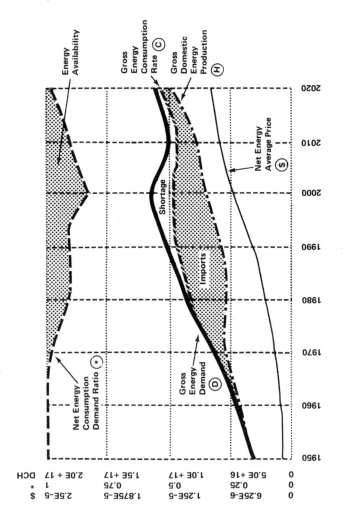

Source: FOSSIL1 model output.

FIGURE 5.2

Business-as-Usual (Scenario) Projection of the Behavior of the U.S. Economy

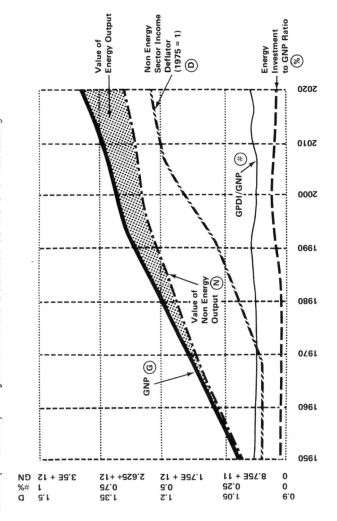

Source: ECONOMY1 model output.

151

FIGURE 5.3

Behavior of the U.S. Energy System in the Low-Price Scenario

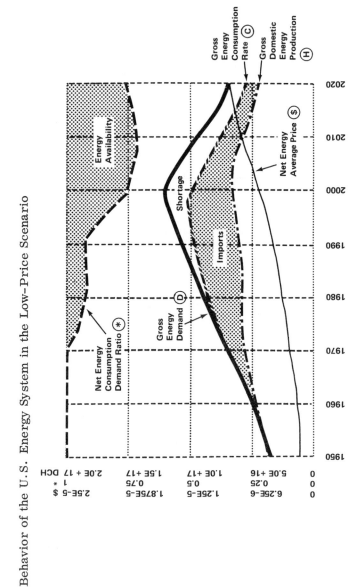

Source: FOSSIL1 model output.

152

FIGURE 5.4

Behavior of the U.S. Economy in the Low-Price Scenario

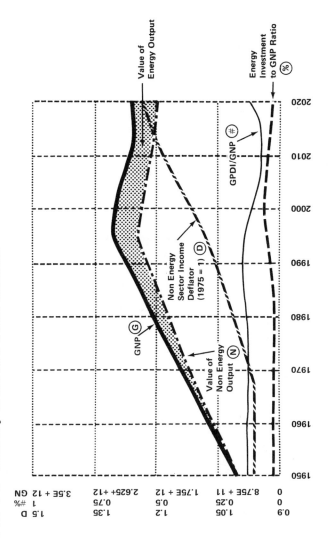

Source: ECONOMY1 model output.

153

FIGURE 5.5

Behavior of the U.S. Energy System in the High–Price Scenario

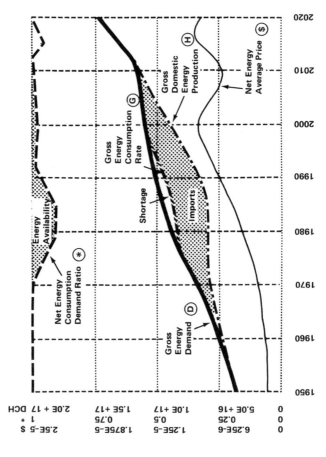

Source: FOSSIL1 model output.

154

FIGURE 5.6

Behavior of the U.S. Economy in the High-Price Scenario

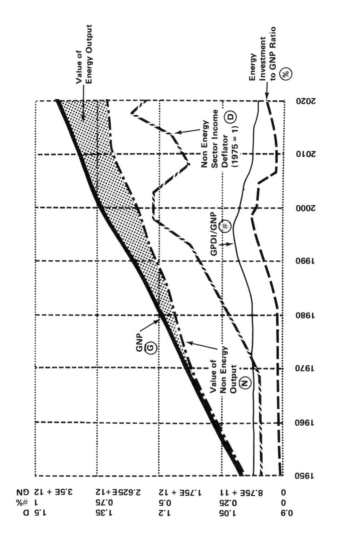

Source: ECONOMY1 model output.

FIGURE 5.7

Behavior of the U.S. Energy System in the Accelerated-Conservation Scenario

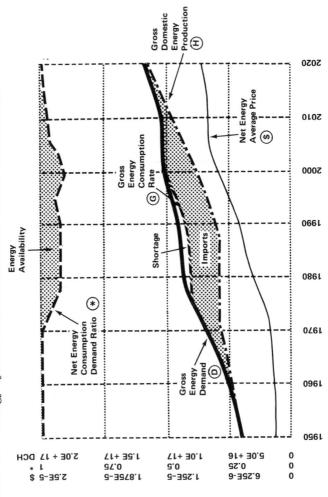

Source: FOSSIL1 model output.

FIGURE 5.8

Behavior of the U.S. Economy in the Accelerated-Conservation Scenario

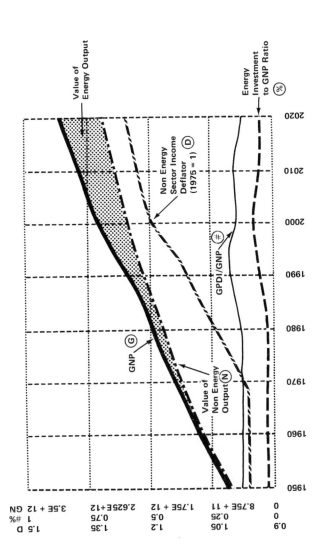

Source: ECONOMY1 model output.

value share of the gross national product rises faster than the value
of nonenergy output of goods and services. The average annual
growth rate in GNP is approximately 1.5 percent between the years
1975 and 2020. This implies a 57 percent reduction in the growth
rate compared to the historical rate of 3.5 percent per year. Furthermore, due to a lack of adequate incentives, domestic energy production grows extremely slowly, causing dependency on imported oil
and increasing susceptibility to world oil shortages. In summary,
the business-as-usual scenario is characterized by high imports
until the turn of the century, persistent shortages, a low growth
rate in nonenergy output, and relatively high energy prices. In
general, the prospects are not too sanguine.

    Figures 5.3 and 5.4 show the low-price scenario projections.
In this scenario, the average energy price rises at a slower rate
than in the business-as-usual scenario. Due to the low OPEC oil
prices assumed in this scenario, the consumption of imports rises,
causing severe shortages in the long run due to the depletion of
world oil resources. The energy shortage effects dominate this
scenario. After the year 2000, the magnitude of shortages exceeds
25 percent and causes a downturn in the economy due to reduced
capacity utilization of nonenergy factors. The trade-off between the
short-term welfare of consumers and the long-term performance of
the economy is clearly illustrated here. The results imply that if
consumerists had their way, then for relatively minor reductions in
the short-run energy prices consumers would be worse off in the
long run due to severe shortages and the consequent dislocations in
the economy.

    Figures 5.5 and 5.6 show the model output in a high-price
scenario. Deregulation policies cause the average energy price to
rise faster than in the business-as-usual scenario. The rise in
energy price stimulates domestic production, causing the imports
and shortages to be far less than in the reference case. For instance,
the energy shortages disappear by 1990, and thus insulate the domestic economy from the effects of world oil depletion. Furthermore,
the imports reach a zero level by the year 2000 and thereby help
achieve the energy self-sufficiency goal of this nation. The deregulation policies, however, cause over-capitalization in the energy
sector by 2000 and generate an oscillatory behavior of energy
prices. This behavior is somewhat analogous to the commonly
observed commodity cycles, which are due to the free market interactions of supply and demand with lags in production capacity acqui-
sition and demand response. The gross national product, in the
high-price scenario, grows at approximately 2 percent per year
after 1975.

The policies implemented in the high-price scenario improve the behavior of the energy-economy system by reducing imports and shortages and causing a higher growth rate of the gross national product compared to the reference run.

Figures 5.7 and 5.8 show the accelerated-conservation scenario runs. The energy-economy system behavior in this scenario is quite similar to the previous case, except for the oscillatory price behavior. The average energy price rises until the year 2000, and then reaches a stable level. The energy shortages are less severe than in the case of the business-as-usual scenario. The imports are reduced to a very low level by the year 2010. In every respect the accelerated conservation case emerges as the most stable of the three scenarios in terms of improvements over the reference case or the business-as-usual scenario.

Except for the price fluctuations, there is, however, a close correspondence between the high-price and the accelerated-conservation scenarios. A strong argument could be made in favor of the conservation scenario over the high-price scenario due to the avoidance of price fluctuations in the energy sector. For example, from a consumer's viewpoint, fluctuating prices may be less desirable than stable levels. Furthermore, deregulation of oil and gas prices would cause over-capitalization in the energy sector, which would be wasteful of resources at a time when they would most likely be needed for other sectors.

In summary, the ecologists' viewpoint of conservation gains more support on the basis of the ECONOMY1 and FOSSIL1 models than the other two, in terms of reducing shortages and imports, and aiding economic growth.

ENERGY AND EQUITY

At first it may seem inappropriate to study the income distributional effects of energy prices with the aid of a highly aggregated model such as ECONOMY1. There is, however, a sufficient richness of detail in the model, of aggregate variables, to allow one to make cautious interpretations regarding the equity issue. In this section the impacts of rising energy prices on two specific groups in the economy are considered.

First, the plight of the worst-off economic group is addressed. Equity is a complex issue and eludes precise definition for objective analysis. Here, the worst-off group is chosen on the basis of John Rawls' difference principle, which suggests that maximizing the welfare of the worst-off individual is a just and fair goal for a

TABLE 5.2

Average Annual Income and Direct Energy Expenditures of Families in the United States, by Income Class, 1972-73 (in dollars)

Income Class by Before-Tax Income	Average After-Tax Annual Income	Annual Expenditures for Household Fuels and Utilities*	Average Annual Expenses for Gasoline and Motor Oil	Total Energy Expenses as a Percent of After-Tax Income
Less than 3,000	1,636	217.88	102.96	19.6
3,000-3,999	3,347	259.76	143.07	12.0
4,000-4,999	4,252	284.00	177.75	10.9
5,000-5,999	5,084	315.23	222.43	10.6
6,000-6,999	5,928	329.46	250.06	9.7
7,000-7,999	6,715	342.53	282.31	9.3
8,000-9,999	7,911	356.69	333.18	8.7
10,000-11,999	9,491	412.67	385.17	8.4
12,000-14,999	11,485	457.55	441.14	7.8
15,000-19,999	14,541	521.49	495.43	7.0
20,000-24,999	18,370	568.12	553.85	6.1
Above 25,000	30,461	684.60	570.17	4.1

*Composed of expenses for electricity, piped gas, bottled gas, fuel oil, kerosene, coal, wood, and other.

Source: U.S. Department of Labor, Bureau of Labor Statistics, Consumer Expenditure Survey Series: Interview Survey, 1972-1973, Report 455-4 (Washington, D.C.: 1977), pp. 5-9.

political economy.[3] For instance, if an energy policy causes a
deterioration of the status of the worst-off groups in the future, then
the policy is considered to be inequitable.

The worst-off group is assumed to consist of the low income
groups such as the poor who are on welfare, the elderly who live on
meager Social Security and pension income, and the unskilled laborers who earn pittances. A recent survey (results of which are tabu-
lated in Table 5.2) suggests that the lowest income class, with less
than $3,000 annual income per family in 1973, required roughly 20 per-
cent of their income for direct energy expenditures. In contrast,
the high income groups, earning over $50,000 annually, spent less
than 5 percent of their income for direct energy uses. The direct
uses consist of gasoline, electricity, heating oil, natural gas, wood,
and propane.

In addition to the direct use of energy, the poor must pay for
the energy content of the basic products they consume. These are
the indirect energy costs. For example, a recent study suggests
that the indirect energy use is higher than the direct use for all
income groups (see Figure 5.9).[4] Thus, if the average energy price
triples over the next two decades, then the low income groups will
have to spend over 70 percent of their income on direct and indirect
energy uses, unless transfer payments offset the increase in energy
costs. But transfer payments would face a stiff political opposition
in a low-growth economy.[†] For instance, in a low-growth economy,
transfer payments to low income groups could not be made without
impairing the standard of living of the higher income groups. Thus,
in order to analyze the impact of higher energy costs on low income
groups, two criteria variables were chosen from the ECONOMY1
model. These are the real income per capita and the fraction of
real income spent on energy for both direct and indirect uses. These
per capita variables indicate the plight of a hypothetical average individual in the economy. The assumption used in selecting these variables is that if the average individual is worse off in the future, then
the worst-off individual today would be much worse off in the future.
Thus, the fraction of real income spent on energy is used here as
an index of the impact of energy costs on disposable income. The
behavior of the real income per capita provides a meaningful measure
of the prospects for increasing the transfer payments to the poor.

---

†Such opposition is already becoming evident, as seen in the
tax referendum in California recently, and the concept of limiting
welfare programs is gaining wide support across the nation.

FIGURE 5.9

Direct and Indirect Household Energy Use, by Income Group

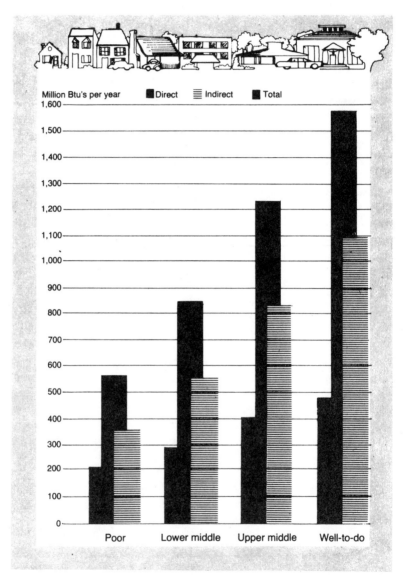

Note: Direct includes only natural gas, electricity, and gasoline

Source: Ford Foundation, A Time to Choose: America's Energy Future (Cambridge, Mass.: Ballinger, 1974), p. 127. Reprinted with permission of the Ford Foundation.

FIGURE 5.10

Sources of Money Income and Distribution of Families in the
United States, by Income Class, 1975

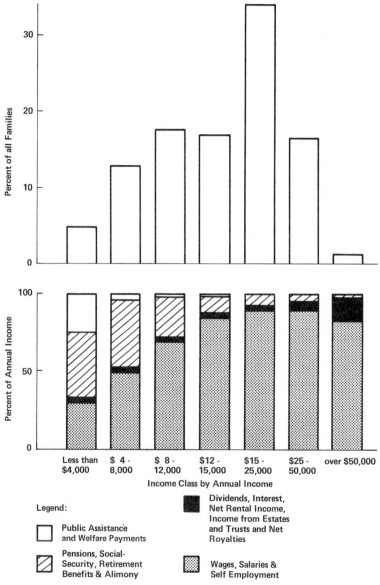

Source: Based on data from U.S. Bureau of the Census, Current
Population Reports, Consumer Income, Series P-60, No. 105
(Washington, D.C., June 1977), p. 40.

FIGURE 5.11

Behavior of Per Capita Variables in the Business–as–Usual Scenario

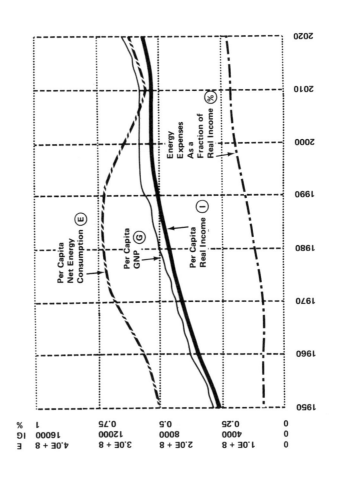

Source: ECONOMY1 model output.

164

FIGURE 5.12

Distribution of Gross National Income in the Business-as-Usual Scenario

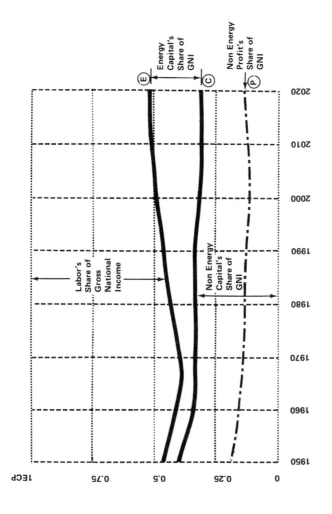

Source: ECONOMY1 model output.

For example, if the growth in real income per capita slows down in the future, then it will become increasingly difficult to raise welfare payments to the poor.

The second group considered in this section is the middle income class. The middle income groups neither qualify for welfare nor have the advantages of capital ownership. Figure 5.10 shows the source of income and the present distribution of families by income class for the year 1975. Over 60 percent of all the families in the United States belong to the middle income group, earning between $8,000 and $25,000 per year. For these families roughly 90 percent of income comes from wages and salaries alone. In contrast, the low income groups receive over 20 percent of their income as transfer payments and the high income groups receive over 13 percent of their income from capital assets. Thus, the future course of functional distribution of income provides one possible measure of the welfare of middle income families who depend mostly on wages and salaries for a living. Historical evidence indicates that there is an inverse relationship between movements in capital to output ratio and movements in labor's share of national income. [5] Since a decline in factor productivity in the energy sector may contribute to an increase of the capital to output ratio for the overall economy in the future, there is clearly a prospect of a declining share of national income to labor. Further, if it is assumed that the capital ownership pattern will not change significantly from its present state, then a decline in labor's share of national income combined with a low growth in national product is bound to leave the middle income groups worse off in the future. This is clearly a politically explosive prospect, considering that the middle income groups constitute a majority of the voting population. Hence, the functional distribution of national income is chosen here as one of the indicators of welfare of the middle income groups.

Furthermore, the equity issue considered here not only concerns the plight of the low and middle income groups but also that of capital owners in the nonenergy sector—such as farmers, homeowners, and stockholders in nonenergy industries. Rising energy costs have adverse effects on profits derived from capital ownership.

Figures 5.11 and 5.12 show the reference projection (business-as-usual scenario) of the distributional variables. The per capita real income levels off after 1990. At the same time, the fraction of real income spent on energy rises from 9 percent in 1975 to 24 percent in 2020. This implies a significant reduction in the standard of living for all income groups, and in particular, for low income groups who would be much worse off than the average individual in the economy. The leveling-off of real income per capita suggests that transfer payments for the poor may be hard to come by.

Furthermore, labor's share of gross national income declines from 61 percent in 1975 to 50 percent in 2010. This reduction in labor's share coupled with the leveling-off of the real income per capita implies serious dislocations in life styles for the low and the middle income groups in the country.

The share of gross national income that goes to energy capital owners in the form of rentals, depreciation, and profits rises from approximately 9 percent in 1975 to over 20 percent by the year 2010. Such a rise implies a squeeze of the income share to nonenergy capital owners, as seen in Figure 5.12. The main reason for the rise in overall capital's share of income is that the capital intensity in the economy is rising, due to substitution of capital for energy as well as labor, and due to a declining productivity of capital in the energy sector from depletion of oil and gas.

Figures 5.13 and 5.14 show the low-price scenario runs. The rise in energy expenses as a fraction of real income in this scenario is at a much lower rate than in the reference scenario. This implies a considerable triumph for the consumerist's cause. The per capita real income, however, declines in the long run for the same reasons as the decline in gross national product which was discussed in the last section. For instance, the shortage effects have a dominant influence over the behavior of the system in the low-price scenario. The per capita net energy consumption declines after 1990, primarily due to the decline in nonenergy capital stock.

The distribution of gross national income is slightly better in the low-price scenario, compared to the reference run, due to a smaller share of income to the energy sector. In this scenario, the energy sector's share of income is approximately 16 percent of the gross national income, compared to 24 percent in the reference scenario. The nonenergy sector profit's share, however, declines due to reduced capacity utilization caused by energy shortages. For example, when capital stock is not utilized to its full capacity, output declines faster than the fixed costs of capital, and thus causes the profits to decline.

The high-price scenario runs are shown in Figures 5.15 and 5.16. Energy expenses as a fraction of real income rise at a faster rate than in the low-price scenario. This fraction reaches a level of 25 percent by the year 2000 from its current level of 9 percent. There is a steady rise in per capita real income due to increased growth in gross output. Labor's share of gross national income, however, declines at a much faster rate than in the reference scenario. By the year 2000 labor's share is reduced to 50 percent from its current level of 61 percent.

Per capita net energy consumption levels off after 1980, due to price-induced conservation. It begins to rise after 2010, due to

FIGURE 5.13

Behavior of Per Capita Variables in the Low–Price Scenario

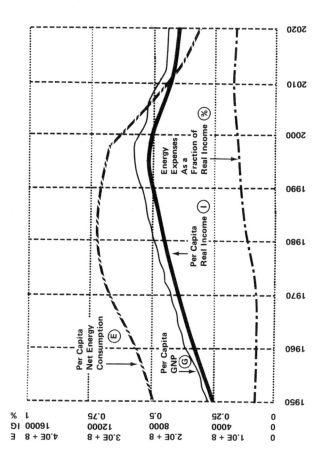

Source: ECONOMY1 model output.

FIGURE 5.14

Distribution of Gross National Income in the Low-Price Scenario

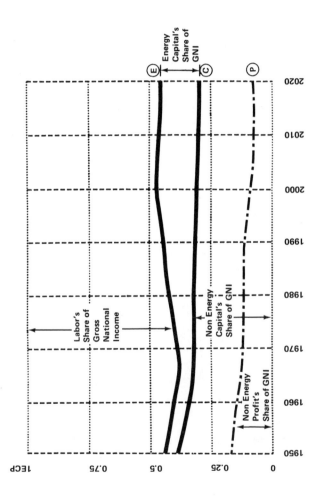

Source: ECONOMY1 model output.

FIGURE 5.15

Behavior of Per Capita Variables in the High-Price Scenario

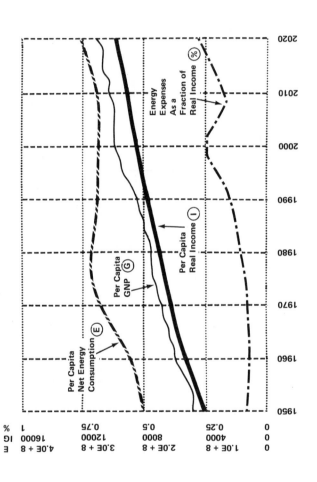

Source: ECONOMY1 model output.

FIGURE 5.16

Distribution of Gross National Income in the High–Price Scenario

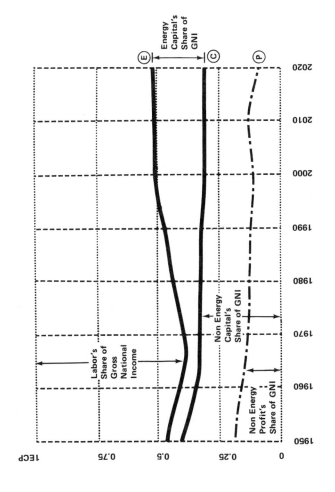

Source: ECONOMY1 model output.

FIGURE 5.17

Behavior of Per Capita Variables in the Accelerated-Conservation Scenario

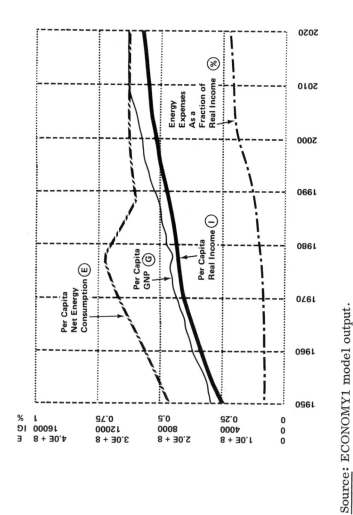

Source: ECONOMY1 model output.

172

FIGURE 5.18

Distribution of Gross National Income in the Accelerated–Conservation Scenario

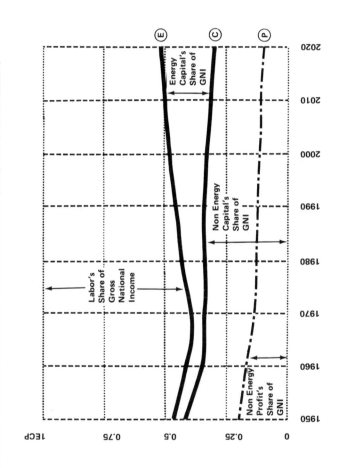

Source: ECONOMY1 model output.

TABLE 5.3

Summary of Results from Alternative Scenario Runs

Year	Gross National Product (trillions of 1975 dollars)	Net Energy Demand (quads)	Energy Shortage (percent)	Oil Imports (quads)	Real Income Per Capita (1975 dollars)	Energy Costs as a Percent of Real Income	Labor's Share of GNP (percent)	Return on Nonenergy Capital (percent)	Nonenergy Capital's Share of GNP (percent)
					Reference Run (BAU)				
1975*	1.52	57.5	0	13	7,500	9	61	11	30
1985	1.94	72.5	9	33	7,660	12	56	10	33
2000	2.42	79.5	17	25	8,380	19	52	7	31
2020	2.98	75.9	2	3	9,190	22	49	9	31
					Low-Price Run				
1985	1.94	72.5	9	33	7,660	12	56	10	33
2000	2.31	84.6	24	28	7,980	16	53	6	32
2020	2.13	52.6	25	9	6,600	16	56	8	28
					High-Price Run				
1985	1.88	72.0	10	31	7,400	14	57	9	33
2000	2.60	75.7	2	14	8,860	24	49	8	30
2020	3.30	92.0	0	0	10,000	25	47	7	31
					Accelerated-Conservation Run				
1985	1.85	66.0	9	27	7,250	12	59	9	34
2000	2.44	71.4	9	18	8,430	20	53	7	32
2020	3.10	77.2	0	0	9,370	24	49	8	30

* Actual values

Source: ECONOMY1 model output.

174

the full realization of the conservation potential. The oscillatory behavior of energy price causes the energy-expenses fraction and profit's share of income to oscillate after the year 2000.

Although, from an economic growth viewpoint, the high-price scenario seems to lead to a desirable behavior of the energy-economy system, from a distributional point of view it emerges as unattractive, due to the faster rise in energy price. Furthermore, the increased growth rate in the gross national product in the high-price scenario is rather deceptive, since most of the increase could be attributed to the value share of energy output. Thus, from an overall viewpoint, the only remaining virtues of the high-price scenario are the reduction in shortages and energy imports. If these were the most dominant concerns of policy makers, then the policies of deregulation associated with the high-price scenario gain support. But from considerations of equity, and hence political feasibility, the high-price scenario policies seem unattractive, since the middle income groups would be penalized largely, due to a reduced share of income to labor.

The accelerated-conservation runs are shown in Figures 5.17 and 5.18. The striking difference in behavior of energy consumption per capita, which levels off by 1990 at its 1965 level of 250 million Btus per year, after a sharp decline due to accelerated conservation measures, implies a low energy-intensive economy. The per capita real income rises almost as fast as in the high-price scenario, and furthermore, there is an extremely gradual rise in the energy expenses fraction. Also, labor's share of gross income declines much more gradually than in the high-price scenario.

Even in the accelerated-conservation scenario, the share of income to labor is eventually reduced to 50 percent of the gross national income. The implication of this reduction is that the behavior of distributive shares is quite insensitive to all policy assumptions considered in this section. The inference to be drawn from this is that the energy sector, due to its capital-intensive nature, adversely affects the rest of the economy by creating severe distributional inequities.

Table 5.3 shows a set of selected critical variables for the years 1985, 2000, and 2020, in the four different scenarios considered in this section. This table is intended for a summary comparison of the four scenarios, in terms of the trade-offs between energy goals and economic goals. The absolute values of the numerical predictions in this table are less important than the relative magnitudes.

The table includes a measure of the return on nonenergy capital (nonenergy profits divided by the capital) that was not shown elsewhere in the plotted outputs. A cursory inspection of this variable suggests that in all the scenarios presented here, there is a secular decline in profitability. Part of this could be attributed to rising energy costs, and the rest to what is commonly known as the capital-deepening effect. † The capital-deepening process could be attributed to the assumption of diminishing rise in productivity and the slow growth rate in population.

The declining return on capital implies that it is not only the low and middle income groups that may be adversely affected in the future, but also the capital owners in the nonenergy sector of the economy. A good example is the domestic agricultural sector. Independent farmers who have no control over the price of their output may be caught in a profit squeeze due to rising costs of energy inputs. The logical consequence would be that farming would become less and less attractive in the future, causing a decline in the farm output. Thus, the secondary and tertiary effects of adverse income distribution may be reduced growth rate of future national output, especially in strategically important sectors such as agriculture.

Any solution to the income distribution problem calls for an increasingly larger role of government as a transfer agent. Thus, the solution may not be politically feasible, and even if feasible, it may only lead to yet another problem of highly centralized and inefficient bureaucracies.

Therefore, in designing a fair and equitable solution to the energy problem, it may be useful to view it as a symptom of an underlying deep-rooted cause—the encouragement of the intensive use of capital in the domestic production processes. An investigation of this cause and a possible solution are addressed in the next section.

AN ALTERNATE SCENARIO

One of the major features of public policy in this country, during the last three decades, has been the encouragement of capital-intensive production processes. During a period of rapid technological change and growing population, the 1950s and the 1960s, policies such as investment tax credits and accelerated depreciation were highly appropriate in promoting economic growth. But in recent times, the character of the U.S. economy has changed considerably. The present economic climate is characterized, for instance, by a declining growth rate in productivity and population. Furthermore,

---

†Capital deepening means that for a given level of labor force and technology (productive efficiency), any additions to capital will reduce profitability. [6]

environmental and safety problems and the depletion of finite
resources such as oil and gas are exacerbating the productivity
problem. In such an economy, it would be counterproductive to
encourage capital-intensive means of production, since this creates
a need for continuously increasing subsidies to offset the diminishing
returns to capital.[†] Moreover, as illustrated in the preceding section, rising capital intensity creates adverse distributional effects.

Considering the persistence of high unemployment rates in
this country, it seems reasonable to assume that labor is somewhat
of an underutilized resource. Thus, it is only logical for the U.S.
government to provide incentives that move the economy toward a
labor-intensive state. This would not only ameliorate the problem
of diminishing profitability, but also reduce the demand for energy.
Also, as one would suppose, the consequences of reduced energy
use would tend to create a better distribution of income compared
to the projections in the preceding section, since there would be
less need for a highly capital-intensive, wealth-concentrating energy
production sector.

For lack of adequate details in the ECONOMY1 model, a
rather simple test is shown in this section, purely for the purpose
of illustrating the effects of a labor-intensive scenario. There are
several ways in which this test could be performed, using the
ECONOMY1 model. For example, the rental rate on capital could
be raised, or the desired profit rate could be increased in a certain
future year during the model run. The latter alternative was chosen
simply for convenience. Thus, for testing the model behavior under
a labor-intensive scenario, the normal profit rate in the nonenergy
sector was changed from 12 percent to 20 percent in 1980.[‡]

Before considering the policy runs that result from this change,
it is useful to review the reference behavior of the model. Figure
5.19 shows the reference behavior of the economy, along with the
movement in capital to labor ratio. The capital to labor ratio rises
until the year 2000 and declines slightly before it levels off by the
year 2020. The behavior of the capital/labor ratio is governed by
substitution mechanisms in ECONOMY1, which respond to rising
relative labor and energy costs. The substitution mechanisms in

---

[†]Recent proposals in Congress to reduce the corporate income
tax rate in order to promote a higher rate of capital formation may
be implicitly due to the pressures caused by diminishing returns to
capital.

[‡]This is analogous to removing partly existing subsidies for
capital formation.

FIGURE 5.19

Reference Projection Showing the Behavior of the Capital to Labor Ratio

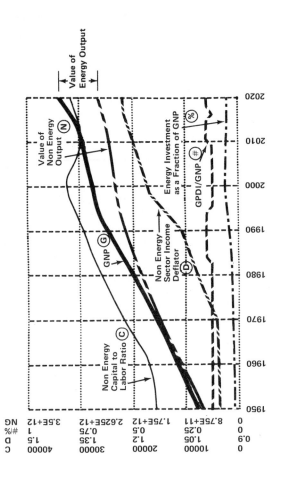

Source: ECONOMY1 model output.

the model cause an increase in the investment rate in nonenergy capital and thus increase the capital/labor and capital/energy ratios.

Another important mechanism in the model that influences the capital to labor ratio is the realized return on nonenergy capital. As the discrepancy between the realized and the actual return increases, investment rate changes to reduce the gap. For example, if the realized return is less than the actual, then the investment rate decreases, and thus causes the profit rate to rise. Since population is exogenous to the model, the movement in the capital investment rate also governs the movement in the capital/labor ratio. Thus, when the desired rate of return is increased in the model, the investment rate falls, causing the capital to labor ratio to decline.

Although several tests were made using the labor-intensive scenario in combination with those discussed previously, only two are reported here in detail. Figures 5.20, 5.21, 5.22, and 5.23 show the model runs illustrating the effects of the high-price scenario in a labor-intensive economy. There is a noticeable improvement in the behavior of distributional variables such as energy expenses as a fraction of real income and labor's share of the gross national income, compared to the high-price scenario runs shown in the last section. The capital to labor ratio begins to decline after 1982 and reaches a stable level until 2015, when it again starts to rise due to induced oscillations from the energy prices. A sharp drop in the ratio of gross private domestic investment to gross national product is seen after 1980, due to the higher desired profit rate implemented in the model. Most important, the desirable characteristics of the high-price scenario, such as low energy imports and shortages, are retained by implementing a labor-intensive economy while considerable improvement of the distributional variables is realized.

Figures 5.24, 5.25, 5.26, and 5.27 show similar test runs for the accelerated-conservation scenario. The per capita energy consumption declines by 1990 to the 1950 level of 200 million Btus per year and remains stable throughout the time horizon. There are significant reductions in the energy sector's share of income compared to the model runs under a pure accelerated-conservation scenario. As in the high-price case, in a labor-intensive economy the accelerated-conservation scenario turns out to be more attractive than before.

Table 5.4 shows a summary of the results from the four different scenarios in a labor-intensive economy. From this table it is evident that, to a policy maker concerned with solving the energy shortage and import problems in an equitable manner,

FIGURE 5.20

The High-Price Scenario Runs in a Labor-Intensive Economy:
the Energy Sector

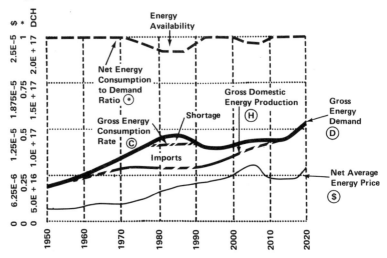

Source: FOSSIL1 model output.

FIGURE 5.21

The High-Price Scenario Runs in a Labor-Intensive Economy:
the Economy

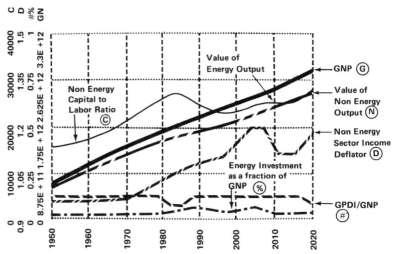

Source: ECONOMY1 model output.

FIGURE 5.22

The High-Price Scenario Runs in a Labor-Intensive Economy:
Per Capita Variables

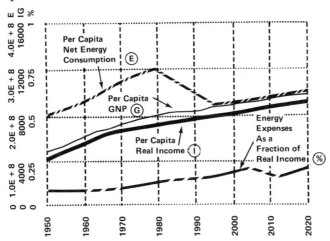

Source: ECONOMY1 model output.

FIGURE 5.23

The High-Price Scenario Runs in a Labor-Intensive Economy:
Distribution of Gross National Income

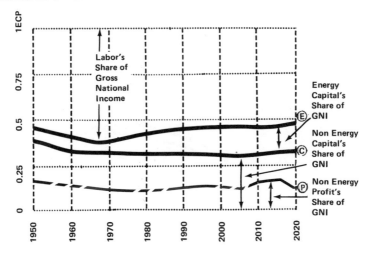

Source: ECONOMY1 model output.

181

FIGURE 5.24

The Accelerated-Conservation Scenario Runs in a Labor-Intensive
Economy: the Energy Sector

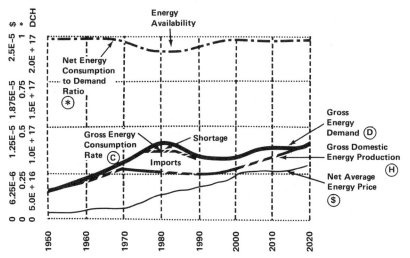

Source: FOSSIL1 model output.

FIGURE 5.25

The Accelerated-Conservation Scenario Runs in a Labor-Intensive
Economy: the Economy

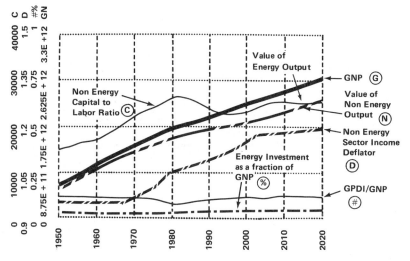

Source: ECONOMY1 model output.

FIGURE 5.26

The Accelerated-Conservation Scenario Runs in a Labor-Intensive
Economy: Per Capita Variables

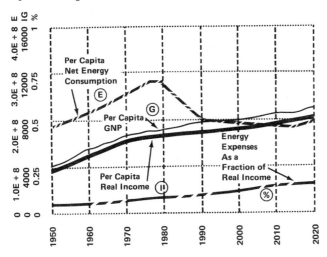

Source: ECONOMY1 model output.

FIGURE 5.27

The Accelerated-Conservation Scenario Runs in a Labor-Intensive
Economy: Distribution of Gross National Income

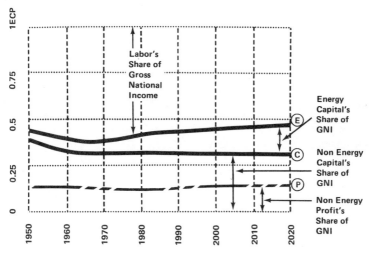

Source: ECONOMY1 model output.

TABLE 5.4

Summary of Results from Alternative Test Scenarios in a Labor-Intensive Economy

Year	Gross National Product (trillions of 1975 dollars)	Net Energy Demand (quads)	Energy Shortage (percent)	Oil Imports (quads)	Real Income Per Capita (1975 dollars)	Energy Costs as a Percent of Real Income	Labor's Share of GNP (percent)	Return on Nonenergy Capital (percent)	Nonenergy Capital's Share of GNP (percent)
				Reference Run (BAU)					
1975*	1.52	57.5	0	13	7,500	9	61	11	30
1985	1.92	70.0	8	31	7,580	12	56	10	33
2000	2.15	64.5	15	21	7,590	15	55	11	31
2020	2.42	56.2	10	6	7,600	15	55	14	31
				Low-Price Run					
1985	1.92	70.0	8	31	7,580	12	56	10	33
2000	2.15	66.0	17	22	7,570	13	55	11	32
2020	2.10	47.4	23	8	6,500	12	59	13	30
				High-Price Run					
1985	1.86	70.0	9	29	7,310	13	58	9	33
2000	2.25	60.0	1	9	7,880	18	54	13	31
2020	2.90	75.0	0	1	8,980	21	50	11	31
				Accelerated-Conservation Run					
1985	1.83	64.0	8	25	7,200	11	60	10	34
2000	2.20	52.3	1	9	7,650	15	56	13	32
2020	2.70	58.5	0	0	8,400	17	53	13	32

* Actual values

Source: From ECONOMY1 and FOSSIL1 model outputs.

encouraging conservation and increased use of labor would be the most rational course of action.

Comparing the results in Tables 5.3 and 5.4, it is seen that there is approximately a 14 percent reduction in gross national product in the year 2020 due to a labor-intensive economy. Labor's share of income, however, is increased by 8 percent. This suggests that in the future there may be a trade-off between economic growth and equity unless there is a significant change in the distribution of wealth. Given that such a change in wealth distribution may be too much to expect, the best alternative may be to sacrifice some growth for the sake of a more equitable distribution of income. On this basis, the policies aimed at encouraging a labor-intensive economy may be justified.

Although no specific translation of the labor-intensive policy option into implementable programs is provided here, a set of general guidelines would easily be developed. For example, the present incentives such as investment tax credits could be modified to encourage the use of more labor. Biasing tax credits in favor of service industries, which tend to be generally more labor-intensive, would be one possible alternative. In many cases, a stiff tax on energy use would in itself promote substitution of labor for capital. This is especially true in the case of short-distance transportation, where bicycles would be substituted for automobiles. For long-distance travel, mass transit would become more attractive. Perhaps the ideal policy would be to remove all types of subsidies that encourage capital accumulation and thus let the free markets determine the rental cost of capital.

A labor-intensive economy calls for considerable change in people's life-styles. Just as a capital-intensive economy causes a high degree of centralization and interdependency among diverse geographical regions, a labor-intensive economy would emphasize decentralization and regional self-sufficiency. Whether such an outcome is desirable or not could be viewed as a matter of individual choice. Beyond that, it is a moral issue concerning what is to be left for posterity. The options are either a highly capital-intensive, sustainable, and more equitable economy. Just as oil and gas price regulation implemented in the thirties and the fifties determined the course of the U.S. economy in the seventies, the energy policies implemented today will largely govern the course of the U.S. economy thirty to fifty years hence.

CONCLUSIONS

The most important conclusion that emerges from this study is that any conceivable solution to the domestic energy problem of high imports and the possibility of shortages points to severe distributional inequities in the future. It is conventional wisdom that distribution is an ethical issue, and hence, lies outside the solution to the energy problem. But the prospects that rising energy costs will nullify the gains made in this country on the egalitarian front, during the last few decades, makes equity a practical issue.

In a growing economy people tolerate inequities, since the future always seems bright and promising. In a low-growth economy, however, inequities may tend to be amplified. More serious is the problem of progressively worsening prospects of distribution of income, as indicated by the analyses presented in the last few sections. This situation could lead to severe class conflicts and cause discontinuous changes in the sociopolitical system. It is primarily for this reason that equity is a highly relevant issue and requires a great deal of attention among policy makers.

In summary, the policy analyses in the last section indicate that attempts to keep energy prices low in the short term could lead to severe energy shortages in the future; that allowing the free market to solve the energy problem (through deregulation) could be highly successful except for its adverse effects on the distribution of income; that a program that would accelerate the conservation of energy would not only solve the problem of high imports and shortages but would have less adverse effect on the distribution than the other alternatives; that energy conservation alone may be insufficient in the long run in dealing with the distribution problem, and it may require encouragement on the part of government to use more labor and less capital in the domestic production processes; and that a labor-intensive economy, in which energy conservation measures are implemented, may be the best course that can be taken to reduce imports, shortages, and inequities, and further, to improve profitability for capital owners.

It must be pointed out that the policy analyses presented in this chapter are based on a highly aggregated model of the U.S. economy. There is definitely a need for further research in several different areas. On the basis of the present work, three important directions for further research can be established. The first is the study of the equity issue in more detail with a disaggregated model based on income classes. The second area is the impact of energy costs on strategic nonenergy sectors such as transportation and agriculture. This would require a disaggregation scheme based on the type of output such as food and transportation services. The third area of study should be the imports/exports sector of the economy, which would help in analyzing the balance-of-trade problem potentially caused by high imports of oil.

Finally, the primary purpose of this volume is to enhance the quality of the energy debate. Very often, issues that seem to belong to the sidelines may be ignored in policy debates, and this could lead to policies that may cause more severe problems than those they were originally designed to solve. The distributional issue discussed in this chapter is one example. Because the ECONOMY1/FOSSIL1 models allow one to test alternate energy policies and study their logical consequences for economic growth and equity, they serve as useful links in the evolution of the energy policy of the United States.

From a methodological point of view, the ECONOMY1 model provides an alternative to the static neoclassical production models discussed in Chapter 2 of this volume, and the conclusions reached using ECONOMY1 are considerably different from the ones that emerge from the neoclassical models. It is hoped that the present work will stimulate constructive debates, aimed at the exploration of new methods of analyzing energy/economy interactions.

NOTES

1. For a detailed description, see "FOSSIL1 Documentation," Dartmouth System Dynamics Group, Thayer School of Engineering, Dartmouth College, Hanover, New Hampshire, 1977.

2. For a detailed description of the policy testing procedure, see "FOSSIL1 User's Manual" and "FOSSIL1 Technical Appendix," Dartmouth System Dynamics Group, 1977.

3. For an excellent discussion on equitable distributive shares, see John Rawls, A Theory of Justice (Cambridge, Mass.: Harvard University Press, 1971), pp. 258-332.

4. See Ford Foundation, A Time to Choose (Cambridge, Mass.: Ballinger, 1974), p. 127.

5. See, for example, Ernst Helmstädter, "The Long-Run Movement of the Capital-Output Ratio and of Labour's Share," in Models of Economic Growth, ed. James A. Mirrlees and N. H. Stern (New York: Wiley, 1973), pp. 3-17.

6. See, for example, Paul A. Samuelson, Economics (New York: McGraw-Hill, 1973), p. 742.

APPENDIX A

ANALYTICAL DESCRIPTIONS OF THE NEOCLASSICAL METHODS

The Basic Neoclassical Model

Consider a simple, yet accurate, version of the neoclassical model of production. Assume that there exists a production function of the form,

$$Y = F(E, R) \qquad E \geq 0, R \geq 0 \tag{1}$$

where Y is the gross output, E is the energy input, and R represents the nonenergy inputs such as capital, labor, and other materials. Now, assuming that the production function F is homogeneous to the degree one,[†] Euler's theorem could be used to write down Y as

$$Y = (F_E \cdot E) + (F_R \cdot R) \tag{2}$$

where

$$F_E = \frac{\partial Y}{\partial E} \qquad \text{and} \qquad F_R = \frac{\partial Y}{\partial R}$$

Thus F_E and F_R are the marginal products. The production function F is assumed to be continuous and differentiable for all E and R. And the first-order partial derivatives of F with respect to E and R are assumed to be greater than zero and the second-order partial derivatives are assumed to be less than zero. Thus, the production function assures that the law of diminishing marginal returns is satisfied. Figure A.1 shows graphically the implication of this assumption.

On the basis of the neoclassical assumptions of perfect competition in product (Y) and the factor (E, R) markets and profit maximization by firms, it follows that

---

[†]Such an assumption implies that

$$\lambda Y = F(\lambda E, \lambda R)$$

where λ is some arbitrary positive constant.[1]

FIGURE A.1

Relationship between Output and Input to Aggregate Production

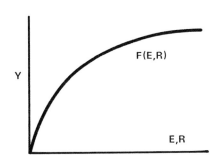

Source: Constructed by the author.

F_E = the unit price of energy and

F_R = the unit price of all other inputs

Thus, the factors of production are rewarded by amounts equal to their marginal products under perfect competition; and an optimal combination of the factors E and R is used by firms to realize maximum profits.

If for some reason (such as depletion) the price of energy rises, the firms change the factor mix in such a manner as to achieve a new optimal combination of E and R. Thus, the production technique will assure that the factor prices are always equal to their marginal products. The degree of substitutability between the factors E and R is measured by the elasticity of substitution σ,[2] which is defined as

$$\sigma = \frac{d \log \frac{R}{E}}{d \log \frac{F_E}{F_R}} \tag{3}$$

This parameter σ is extremely important in determining the impact of the energy sector on the rest of the economy. Its value can range from zero to positive infinity. The value of σ depends on the technology of production. The value of the elasticity-of-substitution

189

parameter does not say anything about the time rate at which substitution occurs, but only about the equilibrium mix of the factors after all transients involved in changing the production process have passed.

At this point it is useful to consider individually the three existing studies, to explore further the neoclassical analysis.

The Energy Modeling Forum Analysis[3] (EMF Study)

The EMF model uses the comparative statics approach to study the sensitivity of the equilibrium value of the gross national product to a change in the availability of energy in the year 2010. Then, the reduction in the assumed GNP in 2000 is computed for various values of the elasticity of substitution between energy and other inputs. The authors of the study first use a static production function model and then a consumer surplus model and arrive at the same conclusions. Here only the production function model is reviewed.

In this study, the aggregate production function is assumed to be of the Constant Elasticity of Substitution (CES) form.[4] Thus:

$$Y^{\frac{\sigma-1}{\sigma}} = a * E^{\frac{\sigma-1}{\sigma}} + b * R^{\frac{\sigma-1}{\sigma}} \tag{4}$$

where

  E = the energy input
  R = the nonenergy input
  Y = the output
  σ = the elasticity of substitution between energy and other
      inputs and $\sigma \neq 0, 1, \infty$
  a, b = the distribution parameters.†

The CES production function is homogeneous to the degree one and thus assumes constant returns to scale (doubling all inputs doubles the output).

The authors of the EMF study assume perfect competition and profit maximization and differentiate Equation (4) with respect to E to arrive at the following relation:[5]

---

†The parameters a and b specify the distributive shares of the output Y among the factors E and R, respectively.

190

$$P_Y \cdot \frac{\partial Y}{\partial E} = P_Y \cdot a \cdot \left(\frac{Y}{E}\right)^{1/\sigma} = P_E \qquad (5)$$

where

P_Y = the unit price of output

P_E = the unit price of energy

From the above equation the demand for energy E is written as

$$E = Y \cdot a^{\sigma} \cdot (P_E/P_Y)^{-\sigma} \qquad (6)$$

The authors treat energy as an intermediate good and assume the value of output to be given by the following relation:†

$$Y = GNP + P_E \cdot E \qquad (7)$$

Further, the authors derive the relations for the distribution parameters in terms of inputs and prices from Equations (4) and (6).[6] Thus, the parameters a and b are given by

$$a = (E_0/Y_0)^{1/\sigma} \cdot P_E^0 \qquad (8)$$

$$b = GNP_0 \cdot (Y_0)^{-1/\sigma} \qquad (9)$$

where the subscript 0 for the variables E, Y, and GNP indicate that they are the base case equilibrium values in the year 2010; and the superscript 0 for the variable P_E indicates the base case value of the energy price.

Now the system equations are fully specified for a comparative static analysis. The EMF computational scheme proceeds as follows:‡

---

†Such a representation is rather confusing, since

$$Y = P_R \cdot R + P_E \cdot E$$

and thus

$$P_R \cdot R = GNP$$

Therefore, the use of empirical values of GNP would involve double counting. It is not clear from the EMF paper how this problem is reconciled.

‡The computational procedure specified here was used to replicate the results of the EMF study.

TABLE A.1

Summary of Results from the Energy Modeling Forum Model

σ	E_{2010} Quads	P_{E}^{2010} (1975 dollars per million Btu)	Change in GNP$_{2010}$ (billions of 1975 dollars)
	220	0.80	0
	190	3.10	-463
0.10	160	11.17	-1856
	110	28.33	-4248
	70	29.85	-4398
	220	0.80	0
	190	1.60	-163
0.20	160	3.49	-490
	110	14.49	-1910
	70	35.32	-3767
	220	0.80	0
	190	1.28	-97
0.30	160	2.18	-254
	110	6.56	-820
	70	20.04	-1976
	220	0.80	0
	190	1.06	-54
0.50	160	1.47	-125
	110	2.97	-320
	70	6.74	-645
	220	0.80	0
	190	0.98	-37
0.70	160	1.24	-82
	110	2.06	-190
	70	3.79	-340

Note: Base Case Assumptions: E_{2010} = 220 quads; GNP$_{2010}$ = 4,400 billion 1975 dollars.

Source: William W. Hogan and Alan S. Manne, "Energy-Economy Interactions: The Fable of the Elephant and the Rabbit?," Energy Modeling Forum Paper, Stanford University, November 1976, p. 18.

Step 1: Assume for the base case,

$$E_0 = E_{2010} = (1.03)^{40} \cdot E_{1970}$$

$$GNP_0 = GNP_{2010} = (1.03)^{40} \cdot GNP_{1970}$$

$$P_E^0 = P_E^{2010} = \$0.80/\text{million Btu}$$

These assumptions are arbitrary and the values of E_0, GNP_0, and P_E^0 turn out to be 220 quadrillion Btus, \$4,400 billion in constant 1975 dollars, and \$0.80 per million Btus, respectively.

Step 2: Assume a value for σ.

Step 3: Find Y_0 from Equation (7) and the parameters a and b from Equations (8) and (9), respectively.

Step 4: Assume an alternate value for E_{2010} and compute the corresponding Y_{2010} from Equation (4), while assuming $R = 1 = $ constant.

Step 5: Solve for the new GNP_{2010} and P_E^{2010} from Equations (8) and (9).

Step 6: Repeat steps 2 through 5 for alternate assumptions of σ and E_{2010}.

The results of the EMF study are summarized in Table A.1. The EMF study tentatively concludes that the value of σ is crucial in assessing the impact of energy prices on future GNP levels, and that σ should be estimated carefully from historical data.[†]

The Institute for Energy Analysis (IEA) Study

In the IEA study,[7] a production function of the following form is assumed:

$$GNP = H \cdot J \cdot \left[\frac{1}{\left(1 + c\,\dfrac{J}{E}\right)} \right] \tag{10}$$

where

[†]The Energy Modeling Forum is involved in comparative analysis of alternative energy-economy models and the study is still under progress.

193

TABLE A.2

Summary of Inputs and Results from the Institute for Energy Analysis Model

Year or Period	GNP*	Internal Growth Rate $\left[\dfrac{\Delta GNP}{GNP}\right]$ (percent)	Labor Force [L]	Labor Productivity Index $\left[\dfrac{GNP}{L} = y\right]$	Internal Growth Rate $\left[\dfrac{\Delta y}{y}\right]$ (percent)	Energy Factor Share $[r_z]$	Energy Price Index $\left[\dfrac{F_z^t}{F_z^{1975}}\right]$
High Energy and Labor, High Prices							
1975	1.172		1.084	1.081		.0226	1.000
1975–1985		3.42					
1985	1.650		1.270	1.299	1.84	.0255	1.533
1985–2000	2.464	2.67	1.440	1.711	1.84	.0292	2.625
2000							
2000–2010	3.100	2.30	1.510	2.053	1.82	.0310	3.539
2010							
1975–2010		2.78			1.83		
High Energy and Labor, Low Prices							
1975	1.180		1.084	1.089		.0159	1.000
1975–1985		3.45					
1985	1.666		1.270	1.312	1.86	.0161	1.228
1985–2000	2.495	2.69	1.440	1.733	1.86	.0171	1.812
2000							
2000–2010	3.145	2.30	1.510	2.083	1.84	.0173	2.218
2010							
1975–2000		2.80			1.85		

Low Energy and Labor, High Prices

1975	1.172	1.084	1.081	1.84	.0227	1.000
1975–1985	3.42					
1985	1.650	1.270	1.299	1.84	.0256	1.519
1985–2000	2.54					
2000	2.416	1.412	1.711	1.82	.0293	2.607
2000–2010	2.08					
2010	2.975	1.449	2.053	1.83	.0311	3.511
1975–2000	2.66					

Low Energy and Labor, Low Prices

1975	1.180	1.084	1.089	1.86	.0159	1.000
1975–1985	3.45					
1985	1.666	1.270	1.312	1.85	.0160	1.218
1985–2000	2.56					
2000	2.446	1.412	1.732	1.85	.0172	1.578
2000–2010	2.16					
2010	3.018	1.449	2.083	1.85	.0173	2.230
1975–2000	2.68					

*Normalized to 1.0 for 1971.

Source: Edward L. Allen et al., U.S. Energy and Economic Growth, Institute for Energy Analysis, Oak Ridge Associated Universities, Oak Ridge, Tennessee, September 1976, p. 150.

195

$H = a \cdot e^{rt}$, the rate of technical change

$J = (b \cdot L^\rho + (1 - b) \cdot K^\rho)^{1/\rho}$, the CES production function with b as the distribution parameter, K as the capital stock, L as the labor force, and ρ as the substitution parameter.

The elasticity of substitution between capital and labor σ[9] is given by

$$\sigma = 1/(1 - \rho) \tag{11}$$

The term $\dfrac{1}{\left(1 + c\dfrac{J}{E}\right)}$ is called the energy deflator by the authors of the IEA study. In this term E is the energy consumed and c is the parameter indicating energy's factor share of the gross national product.

The parameters a, b, ρ, r, and c are estimated from historical data (1929-73) and are shown below.

Parameter	Best Value
a	0.233
b	0.966
c	0.0134
r	0.0180
ρ	-1.256

The authors further assume perfect competition and profit maximization, and hence suggest that the marginal product due to energy equals the energy price, both in the past and in the future. Further, they let $\dfrac{E}{c} = Z$, and take partial derivative of GNP with respect to Z.

$$\frac{\partial (GNP)}{\partial Z} = F_Z = \frac{(J) \cdot (GNP)}{(Z + J) \cdot (Z)} \tag{12}$$

With Equations (10) and (12), the IEA computations are carried out as shown below.[10]

Step 1: Assume the following exogenous inputs:
- labor force L(t) in man-hours available in the year t;
- factor productivity parameter r(t) as estimated from historical data;
- energy consumption E(t) in quads;

- savings rate s and depreciation rate δ;
- energy cost parameter $c(t)$.

Step 2: Find GNP(t) and $F_Z(t)$ (energy price) from Equations (10) and (12).

Step 3: Adjust capital stock for depreciation and investment using the accounting relationship $\Delta K(t) = s \cdot GNP(t) - \delta \cdot K(t)$.

Step 4: Repeat steps 1 through 4 for alternate sets of input variables.

The results of the IEA analysis of four different scenarios are summarized in Table A.2. The four scenarios correspond to assumptions of four different combinations of exogenous inputs of energy consumption $E(t)$, labor force $L(t)$, and energy prices $F_Z(t)$. The first scenario assumes high growth in $E(t)$ and $L(t)$ and the energy price to rise by a factor of 3.5 between 1975 and 2010. The resultant reduction in GNP growth rate is found to be 0.64 percent in the year 2010 from its historical value of approximately 3.5 percent per year. Similarly, the reduction in GNP growth rates is computed for three other scenarios. On the basis of the results indicated in Table A.2, the IEA study concludes that the impact of higher energy prices on the GNP growth rates is too minimal to be of concern.

The Hudson-Jorgenson Study

The Hudson-Jorgenson model[11] of energy/economy interactions is by far the most elaborate of the three models discussed in Chapter 2. In this section, the model purpose, method, and conclusions are reviewed. No attention is paid to the detailed individual equations.[†]

The Hudson-Jorgenson model is designed to assess the impact on the outputs and prices of major nonenergy sectors of the U.S. economy (such as agriculture, nonfuel mining, construction, manufacturing, transportation, communications, trade, and services) of alternate energy conservation measures such as energy taxes and technical fix policies.

[†]The Hudson-Jorgenson model could not be tested independently due to the proprietary nature of the data base that is required for the interindustry model. Thus, the critique here does not address quantitative measures.

FIGURE A.2

A Schematic Diagram of the Hudson-Jorgenson Macroeconomic Growth Model

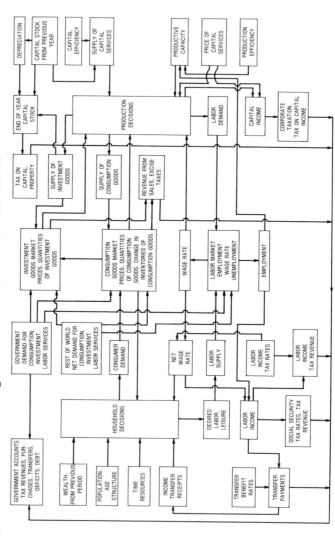

Source: Edward S. Hudson and Dale W. Jorgenson, "U.S. Energy Policy and Economic Growth, 1975–2000," _Bell Journal of Economics and Management Science_ 5 (Autumn 1974): 489. Reprinted with permission.

The model used in this study consists of two major submodels—the macroeconomic growth model and the interindustry input/output model. The macroeconomic growth model is a dynamic, two-sector, neoclassical model of the U.S. aggregate economy with capital, labor, and productivity as primary inputs.[12] The capital goods and the consumption goods sectors constitute the two basic segments of the growth model. The major assumptions that govern the behavior of this model are that households maximize utility by allocating their time between work and leisure and their income between current and future consumption; that firms maximize profits by choosing an optimal combination of capital and labor inputs and enjoy a periodic reward of productivity increases; that the time lags involved in factor substitution processes are too small to have any appreciable effect on the economy; and that perfect competition exists in factor and product markets.

With the help of these assumptions, the growth model is designed to generate equilibrium prices of capital and labor services, the volume of gross private domestic investment, and the value of personal consumption expenditures. These variables are used as inputs to the interindustry model. Figure A.2 shows a schematic diagram of the macroeconomic model. The heart of the model is represented by the two boxes labeled household and production decisions. The decision functions that represent the behavior of these two sectors are based on the maximizing assumptions listed above. The boxes at the center of the diagram represent the supply/demand interactions in the investment goods, consumption goods, and labor markets. These three markets are represented as perfect markets, where prices are determined purely through supply/demand interactions.

The interindustry model consists of nine major sectors, four of which represent the nonenergy sectors and the rest represent the five energy sectors:[13] agriculture, nonfuel mining, and construction; manufacturing, excluding petroleum refining; transportation; communications, trade, and services; coal mining; crude petroleum and natural gas; petroleum refining; electric utilities; and gas utilities.

The interindustry model is set in an input/output framework and the coefficients of the input/output matrix are determined endogenously as a function of four input prices:[14] the price of capital services, the price of labor services, the price of energy (both domestic and imports), and the price of nonenergy materials. The first two of these prices are determined by the macroeconomic model and the rest by the input/output model. The prices of domestic availability of outputs from each of the nine sectors are determined by a simultaneous solution of a set of nine price possibility frontier equations. The price possibility frontiers are simply a set of

FIGURE A. 3

The Hudson-Jorgenson Interindustry Model Computational Scheme

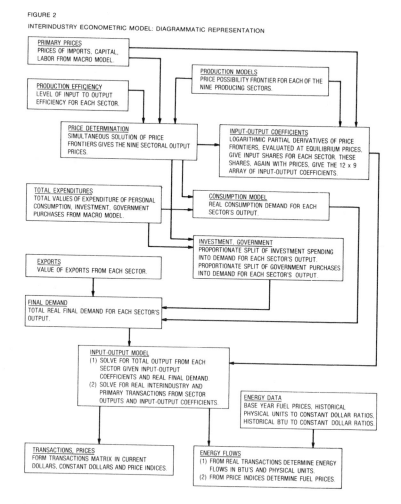

FIGURE 2

INTERINDUSTRY ECONOMETRIC MODEL: DIAGRAMMATIC REPRESENTATION

3. Producer behavior   ■ Our interindustry model includes econometric models of producer behavior for each of the nine industrial sectors included in the model.[12] In implementing an econometric model of producer behavior for each sector our primary objective is to explore the

---

[12] This Section is based on Berndt and Jorgenson [5].

Source: Edward S. Hudson and Dale W. Jorgenson, "U.S. Energy Policy and Economic Growth, 1975-2000," Bell Journal of Economics and Management Science 5 (Autumn 1974): 474. Reprinted with permission.

alternate representations of the production functions for each of the nine sectors in the input/output model. Thus, the disaggregated model presented by Hudson and Jorgenson is essentially a disaggregated version of the basic one-sector neoclassical production model that was presented earlier in this appendix.

Figure A.3 shows a schematic representation of the computational scheme of the interindustry model.[15] This diagram is self-explanatory and clearly specifies the exogenous inputs to the interindustry model. It is interesting to note that the gross private domestic investment generated as an output of the macroeconomic model is allocated exogenously among the nine sectors of the input/output model. In the description of the model the authors give very little justification for this type of allocation procedure. Furthermore, most of the exogenous variables are assumed to continue to be in historical proportions, and the authors do not conduct sensitivity analyses to identify the significance of these assumptions. The model does not address the institutional constraints involved in the substitution of labor for energy. More important, the Hudson-Jorgenson model does not address the issue of domestic oil and gas depletion; that is, the model does not explicitly include a resource sector. Thus, it is not clear from the descriptions how the relative prices of conventional fossil fuels are generated in the model.

The single major conclusion that emerges from the work of Hudson and Jorgenson is that significant reductions in energy consumption could be realized through a tax on energy use, without loss in real income. As the authors state,

> The basic properties of the model are illustrated by the result that, in the 1980 simulations for example, energy input can be reduced by 8 percent at the cost of only a 1-percent increase in average prices and a 0.4-percent decrease in real income. In other words, the flexibility of the economy in adapting to changing resource availabilities, and the power of the price system in securing this adaptation, mean that substantial reductions in energy use can be achieved without major economic cost.[16]

This conclusion is clearly based on one set of behavioral assumptions, which the authors make no attempt to justify. However, if the conclusion remains unchanged under an alternate set of assumptions, then the credibility of the model results among policy makers would be considerably enhanced. Chapter 3 states an alternate set of assumptions, which are later incorporated into a formal representation of the U.S. energy/economy system.

NOTES

1. See, for example, R. G. D. Allen, Macro-Economic Theory (New York: Macmillan, 1968), p. 43; and Milton Friedman, Price Theory (Chicago: Aldine, 1976), pp. 194-96.

2. See Allen, Macro-Economic Theory, p. 48.

3. William W. Hogan and Alan S. Manne, "Energy-Economy Interactions: The Fable of the Elephant and the Rabbit?," Energy Modeling Forum, Stanford University, November 1976.

4. For a description of the CES production function see Kenneth J. Arrow et al., "Capital-Labor Substitution and Economic Efficiency," Review of Economics and Statistics 43 (August 1961): 225-50.

5. Hogan and Manne, "Energy-Economy Interactions," p. 6.

6. See Hogan and Manne, "Energy-Economy Interactions," p. 9, for details of the derivation of the equation for the distribution parameters a and b.

7. Edward L. Allen et al., U.S. Energy and Economic Growth, Institute for Energy Analysis, Oak Ridge Associated Universities, Oak Ridge, Tennessee, September 1976.

8. The rate of technical change is assumed here to be Hick's neutral type, which implies that technical change favors both capital and labor inputs. See Allen, Macro-Economic Theory, p. 248.

9. See, for example, Allen, Macro-Economic Theory, p. 52.

10. See Allen, U.S. Energy and Economic Growth, p. 119.

11. Edward S. Hudson and Dale W. Jorgenson, "U.S. Energy Policy and Economic Growth, 1975-2000," Bell Journal of Economics and Management Science 5 (Autumn 1974).

12. For a description of the two-sector neoclassical growth model, see Allen, Macro-Economic Theory, pp. 220-34; and Edwin Burmeister and Rodney A. Dobell, Mathematical Theories of Economic Growth (New York: Macmillan, 1970), pp. 107-30.

13. See Hudson and Jorgenson, "U.S. Energy Policy and Economic Growth, 1975-2000," p. 481. The authors do not give any justification for choosing nine sectors instead of ten or twelve.

14. See Wassily W. Leontief, The Structure of the American Economy (Oxford: Oxford University Press, 1953), for an exposition of the input/output analysis. Leontief's model uses a static framework where the input/output coefficients are exogenously specified. For a dynamic version, see M. Morishima, "A Dynamic Leontief System with Neo-Classical Production Functions," in Morishima, Equilibrium Stability and Growth (Oxford: Oxford University Press, 1964), pp. 54-92.

15. See Hudson and Jorgenson, "U.S. Energy Policy and Economic Growth, 1975-2000," p. 474.

16. Ibid., p. 512.

APPENDIX B

THE DYNAMO FLOW DIAGRAM OF ECONOMY1

LEGEND   **DYNAMO FLOW DIAGRAM SYMBOLS**

A Level or a Stock Variable

A Rate or Flow Variable

Auxillary Variable

Material Delay

Information Delay

Constant

Conservative Material flows

Non-conservative Information flows

Note: The numbers within each of the symbols denote the
respective equation number in the DYNAMO program.

FIGURE B.1

The DYNAMO Flow Diagram of ECONOMY1

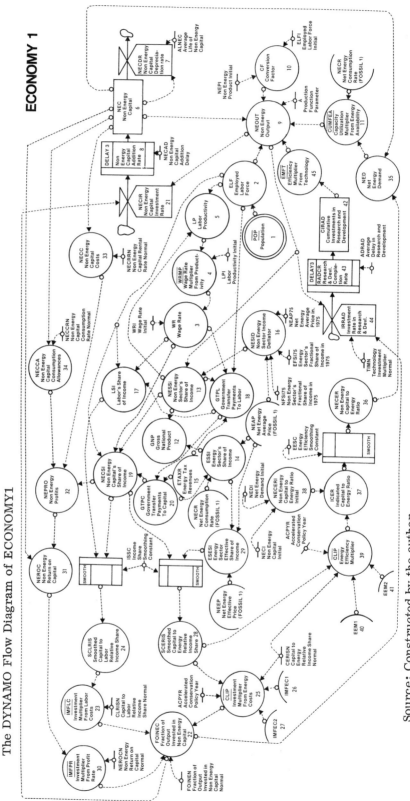

Source: Constructed by the author.

APPENDIX C

LIST OF ECONOMY1 MODEL EQUATIONS

ECONOMY1 06 JUL 77   13:06

```
100 NOTE  ****************************************************
110 NOTE  ****************************************************
120 NOTE  A MODEL OF THE ENERGY ECONOMY INTERACTION
130 NOTE  ****************************************************
140 NOTE  ****************************************************
150 NOTE
160 NOTE  ****************************************************
170 NOTE  POPULATION / LABOR-FORCE SECTOR
180 NOTE  ****************************************************
190 NOTE
200 A  POP.K=TABHL(POPT,TIME.K,1950,2020,19)*1E8
210 T  POPT=1.52/1.81/2.05/2.23/2.45/2.62/2.79/2.94
220 A  ELF.K=POP.K*NFPE
230 C  NFPE=0.4
240 NOTE
250 NOTE  ****************************************************
260 NOTE  LABOR PRODUCTIVITY AND WAGES SECTOR
270 NOTE  ****************************************************
280 NOTE
290 A  WR.K=WRI*WRMP.K
300 C  WRI=6000
310 A  WRMP.K=TABHL(WRMPT,(LP.K/LPI),1,4,0.25)
320 T  WRMPT=1/1.3/1.7/2.05/2.15/2.3/2.5/2.75/3/3.25/3.5/3.75/4
330 A  LP.K=NESSI.K/ELF.K
340 C  LPI=10420
350 NOTE
360 NOTE  ****************************************************
370 NOTE  NON-ENERGY PRODUCTION SECTOR
380 NOTE  ****************************************************
390 NOTE
400 NOTE  NON-ENERGY CAPITAL
410 NOTE
420 L  NEC.K=NEC.J+(DT)(NECAR.JK-NECDR.JK)
430 N  NEC=NECI
440 C  NECI=0.95E12
450 R  NECDR.KL=NEC.K/ALNEC
```

```
460  C  ALNEC=20
470  R  NECAR.KL=DELAY3(NECIR.JK,NECAD)
480  C  NECAD=5
490  NOTE
500  NOTE  NON ENERGY OUTPUT
510  NOTE
520  A  NEOUT.K=(EMFT.K)((NEC.K)^A)((ELF.K)^(1-A))*CF.K*
        CUMFEA.K
530  C  A=0.33
540  A  CF.K=(NEPI)/(((NECI)^A)((ELFI)^(1-A)))
550  C  NEPI=600E9
560  C  ELFI=61E6
570  A  CUMFEA.K=TABHL(CUMFEAT,NECR.K/NED.K,0,1,0.2)
580  T  CUMFEAT=0/0.1/0.3/0.7/0.9/1
590  NOTE
600  NOTE  ***************************************************
610  NOTE  PRODUCT AND INCOME SHARE ACCOUNTING SHARE
630  NOTE
640  A  GNP.K=NESSI.K+ESSI.K
650  A  NESSI.K=NEOUT.K/HESID.K
660  A  ESSI.K=NEAP.K*NECR.K-ETAXR.K
670  A  ETAXR.K=TOXT.K*TOPR.K+TGXT.K*TGPR.K+IOTAR.K*
        IOCR.K
680  A  NESID.K=NFSI75+(NEAP.K/NEAP75)*EFSI75
690  C  NFSI75=0.9
700  C  EFSI75=0.1
710  C  NEAP75=2.5E-06
720  A  LSI.K=WR.K*ELF.K+GTPL.K
730  A  GTPL.K=WR.K*ELF.K*ETAXR.K/NESSI.K
740  A  NECSI.K=NESSI.K-WR.K*ELF.K+GTPC.K
750  A  GTPC.K=ETAXR.K-GTPL.K
760  NOTE
770  NOTE  ***************************************************
780  NOTE  FACTOR SUBSTITUTION AND INVESTMENT SECTOR
790  NOTE  ***************************************************
800  NOTE
810  R  NECIR.KL=NEOUT.K*FOINEC.K
820  A  FOINEC.K=FOINEN*IMFLC.K*IMFEC.K*IMFPR.K
830  C  FOINEN=0.125
840  NOTE
850  NOTE  CAPITAL LABOR SUBSTITUTION
860  NOTE
870  A  IMFLC.K=TABHL(IMFLCT,SCLRIS.K/CLRISN,0,1,0.2)
880  T  IMFLCT=1.1/1.095/1.075/1.025/1.005/1
890  A  SCLRIS.K=SMOOTH(NECSI.K/LSI.K,ISSC)
```

```
900  C  ISSC=5
910  C  CLRISN=0.85
920  NOTE
930  NOTE  CAPITAL ENERGY SUBSTITUTION
940  NOTE
950  A  IMFEC.K=CLIP(IMFEC1.K,IMFEC2.K,TIME.K,ACPYR)
960  A  IMFEC1.K=TABHL(IMFECT1,SCERIS.K/CERISN,0,1,0.2)
970  T  IMFECT1=1.1/1.1/1.095/1.075/1.025/1
980  A  IMFEC2.K=TABHL(IMFECT2,SCERIS.K/CERISN,0,1,0.2)
990  T  IMFECT2=1.1/1.095/1.075/1.025/1.005/1
1000 C  ACPYR=2100
1010 A  SCERIS.K=SMOOTH(NECSI.K/ESESI.K,ISSC)
1020 N  SCERIS=6.8
1030 C  CERISN=6.8
1040 A  ESESI.K=ESSI.K*NEEP.K/NEAP.K
1050 NOTE
1060 NOTE  INVESTMENT MULTIPLIER FROM PROFIT RATE
1070 NOTE
1080 A  IMFPR.K=TABHL(IMFPRT,NEROC.K/NEROCN,0,1.4,0.2)
1090 T  IMFPRT=0/0.1/0.3/0.5/0.9/1/1.1/1.1
1100 C  NEROCN=0.12
1110 A  NEROC.K=NEPRO.K/NEC.K
1120 A  NEPRO.K=NECSI.K-NECC.K-NECCA.K
1130 A  NECC.K=NEC.K*NECRRN
1140 C  NECRRN=0.1
1150 A  NECCA.K=NEC.K*NECCRN
1160 C  NECCRN=0.05
1170 NOTE
1180 NOTE  ****************************************************
1190 NOTE  ENERGY DEMAND SECTOR
1200 NOTE  ****************************************************
1210 NOTE
1220 A  NED.K=NEC.K/NECER.K
1230 A  NECER.K=SMOOTH(ICER.K,EESC)
1240 C  EESC=10
1250 A  ICER.K=NECERI.K*EEM.K
1260 A  NECERI.K=NECI/NEDI
1270 C  NEDI=30E15
1280 A  EEM.K=CLIP(EEM1.K,EEM2.K,TIME.K,ACPYR)
1290 A  EEM1.K=TABHL(EEMT1,SCERIS.K/CERISN,0,1,0.1)
1300 T  EEMT1=1.71/1.71/1.71/1.68/1.6/1.5/1.3/1.05/1.01/1.0/1.0
1310 A  EEM2.K=TABHL(EEMT2,SCERIS.K/CERISN,0,1,0.1)
1320 T  EEMT2=1.71/1.71/1.65/1.5/1.35/1.2/1.05/1.02/1.01/1/1
1330 NOTE
```

```
1340 NOTE ****************************************************
1350 NOTE TECHNOLOGY SECTOR
1360 NOTE ****************************************************
1370 NOTE
1380 L CIRAD.K=CIRAD.J+(DT)(RADCR.JK)
1390 N CIRAD=0
1400 R RADCR.KL=DELAY3(IRRAD.JK,ADRAD)
1410 C ADRAD=10
1420 R IRRAD.KL=FOINEC.K*TIMN*NEOUT.K
1430 C TIMN=0.15
1440 A EMFT.K=TABHL(EMFTT,CIRAD.K,0,2E12,0.125E12)
1450 T EMFTT=1/1.3/1.4/1.5/1.6/1.68/1.76/1.84
1460 X 1.9/1.93/1.96/1.98/1.99/2/2/2/2
1470 NOTE
1480 NOTE SUPPLEMENTARY VARIABLES
1490 NOTE
1500 A NECISF.K=NECSI.K/GNP.K
1510 A ESISF.K=ESSI.K/GNP.K
1520 A LISF.K=LSI.K/GNP.K
1530 A TCISF.K=NECISF.K+ESISF.K
1540 A NI.K=GNP.K-TCCA.K
1550 A TCCA.K=NECCA.K+ECCA.K
1560 A ECCA.K=DONCC.K+TGNCC.K+SENCC.K+DCNCC.K
1570 A GPDI.K=NECIR.JK+EINV.K
1580 A GPDIGF.K=GPDI.K/GNP.K
1590 A EINVGF.K=EINV.K/GNP.K
1600 A EINV.K=DOINV.K+TGINV.K+DCINV.K+SEINV.K
1610 A CONS.K=GNP.K-GPDI.K
1620 A CONSPC.K=(GNP.K-GPDI.K)/POP.K
1630 A ECPC.K=ESSI.K/POP.K
1640 A RIPC.K=NI.K/POP.K
1650 A ECPCF.K=ECPC.K/RIPC.K
1660 A NEPFGN.K=NEPRO.K/GNP.K
1670 A PCNEC.K=NECR.K/POP.K
1680 A GNPPC.K=GNP.K/POP.K
```

APPENDIX D

LIST OF DEFINITIONS OF VARIABLES IN ECONOMY1 MODEL

A	Production Function Parameter	
ACPYR	Accelerated-Conservation Policy Year	(Year)
ADRAD	Average Delay in Research and Development	(Years)
ALNEC	Average Life of Nonenergy Capital Stock	(Years)
CERISN	Capital to Energy Relative Income Share, Normal	(Fraction)
CF	Conversion Factor	
CIRAD	Cumulative Investment in Research and Development	(1975 $)
CLRISM	Capital to Labor Relative Income Share, Normal	(Fraction)
CONS	Consumption	(1975 $/Year)
CONSPC	Consumption Per Capita	(1975 $/Year/Person)
CUMFEA	Capacity Utilization Multiplier from Energy Availability	
CUMFEAT	Capacity Utilization Multiplier from Energy Availability Table	
DCINV	Domestic Coal Investments	(1975 $/Year)
DCNCC	Domestic Coal Noncash Charges	(1975 $/Year)
DOINV	Domestic Oil Investments	(1975 $/Year)
DONCC	Domestic Oil Noncash Charges	(1975 $/Year)
ECCA	Energy Capital Consumption Allowances	(1975 $/Year)
ECPC	Energy Cost Per Capita	(1975 $/Year/Person)
ECPCF	Energy Costs as a Fraction of Real Income	(Fraction)
EEM	Energy Efficiency Multiplier	(Dimensionless)
EEM1	Energy Efficiency Multiplier 1	(Dimensionless)
EEM2	Energy Efficiency Multiplier 2	(Dimensionless)
EEMT1	Energy Efficiency Multiplier Table 1	
EEMT2	Energy Efficiency Multiplier Table 2	
EESC	Energy Efficiency Smoothing Constant	(Years)
EFSI75	Energy Sector Fractional Share of Income, 1975	(Fraction)
EINV	Energy Sector Investments	(1975 $/Year)
EINVGF	Energy Investments to GNP Fraction	(Fraction)
ELF	Employed Labor Force	(People)
ELFI	Employed Labor Force, Initial, 1950	(People/Year)
EMFT	Efficiency Multiplier from Technology	(Dimensionless)
EMFTT	Efficiency Multiplier from Technology Table	

ESESI	Energy Sector Effective Share of Income	(1975 $/Year)
ESISF	Energy Sector Income Share Fraction	(Fraction)
ESSI	Energy Sector Share of Income	(1975 $/Year)
ETAXR	Energy Tax Revenues	(1975 $/Year)
FOINEC	Fraction of Output Invested in Non Energy Capital	(Fraction)
FOINEN	Fraction of Output Invested in Non Energy Capital, Normal	(Fraction)
GNP	Gross National Product	(1975 $/Year)
GNPPC	Gross National Product Per Capita	(1975 $/Person/Year)
GPDI	Gross Private Domestic Investment	(1975 $/Year)
GPDIGF	Gross Private Domestic Investment to GNP Fraction	(Fraction)
GTPC	Government Transfer Payment to Capital	(1975 $/Year)
GTPL	Government Transfer Payment to Labor	(1975 $/Year)
ICER	Indicated Capital to Energy Ratio	(1975 $/Btu/Year)
IMFEC	Investment Multiplier from Energy Costs	(Dimensionless)
IMFEC1	Investment Multiplier from Energy Costs 1	(Dimensionless)
IMFEC2	Investment Multiplier from Energy Costs 2	(Dimensionless)
IMFECT1	Investment Multiplier from Energy Costs Table 1	
IMFECT2	Investment Multiplier from Energy Costs Table 2	
IMFLC	Investment Multiplier from Labor Costs	(Dimensionless)
IMFLCT	Investment Multiplier from Labor Cost Table	
IMFPR	Investment Multiplier from Profit Rate	(Dimensionless)
IMFPRT	Investment Multiplier from Profit Rate Table	
IOCR	Imported Oil Consumption Rate	(Btu/Year)
IOTAR	Import Oil Tariffs	(1975 $/Btu)
IRRAD	Investment Rate in Research and Development	(1975 $/Year)
ISSC	Income Share Smoothing Constant	(Years)
LISF	Labor Income Share Fraction	(Fraction)
LP	Labor Productivity	(1975 $/Man-Year)
LPI	Labor Productivity, Initial, 1950	(1975 $/Man-Year)

LSI	Labor Share of Income	(1975 $/Year)
NEAP	Net Energy Average Price	(1975 $/Btu)
NEAP75	Net Energy Average Price, 1975	(1975 $/Btu)
NEC	Nonenergy Capital Stock	(1975 $)
NECAD	Nonenergy Capital Addition Delay	(Years)
NECAR	Nonenergy Capital Addition Rate	(1975 $/Year)
NECC	Nonenergy Capital Costs	(1975 $/Year)
NECCA	Nonenergy Capital Consumption Allowances	(1975 $/Year)
NECCRN	Nonenergy Capital Consumption Rate, Normal	(Fraction/Year)
NECDR	Nonenergy Capital Depreciation Rate	(1975 $/Year)
NECER	Nonenergy Capital to Energy Ratio	(1975 $/Btu/Year)
NECERI	Nonenergy Capital to Energy Ratio, Initial, 1950	(1975 $/Btu/Year)
NECI	Nonenergy Capital Stock, Initial	(1975 $)
NECIR	Nonenergy Capital Investment Rate	(1975 $/Year)
NECISF	Nonenergy Capital Income Share Fraction	(Fraction)
NECR	Net Energy Consumption Rate	(Btu/Year)
NECRRN	Nonenergy Capital Rental Rate, Normal	(Fraction/Year)
NECSI	Nonenergy Capital Share of Income	(1975 $/Year)
NED	Net Energy Demand	(Btu/Year)
NEDI	Net Energy Demand, Initial, 1950	(Btu/Year)
NEEP	Net Energy Effective Price	(1975 $/Btu)
NEOUT	Nonenergy Output	(1975 $/Year)
NEPFGN	Nonenergy Profits as a Fraction of GNP	(Fraction)
NEPI	Nonenergy Product, Initial, 1950	(1975 $/Year)
NEPRO	Nonenergy Sector Profits	(1975 $/Year)
NEROC	Nonenergy Return on Capital	(Fraction/Year)
NEROCN	Nonenergy Return on Capital, Normal	(Fraction/Year)
NESID	Nonenergy Sector Income Deflator	(Dimensionless)
NESSI	Nonenergy Sector Share of Income	(1975 $/Year)
NFPE	Normal Fraction of Population Employed	(Fraction)
NFSI75	Nonenergy Sector Fractional Share of Income, 1975	(Fraction)
NI	National Income	(1975 $/Year)
PCNEC	Per Capita Net Energy Consumption Rate	(Btu/Person/Year)
POP	Population	(People)
POPT	Population Table	

RADCR	Research and Development Completion Rate	(1975 $/Year)
RIPC	Real Income Per Capita	(1975 $/Year/Person)
SCERIS	Smoothed Capital to Energy Relative Income Share	(Fraction)
SCLRIS	Smoothed Capital to Labor Relative Income Share	(Fraction)
SEINV	Steam Electric Investments	(1975 $/Year)
SENCC	Steam Electric Noncash Charges	(1975 $/Year)
TCCA	Total Capital Consumption Allowances	(1975 $/Year)
TCISF	Total Capital Income Share Fraction	(Fraction)
TGINV	Total Gas Investments	(1975 $/Year)
TGNCC	Total Gas Noncash Charges	(1975 $/Year)
TGPR	Total Gas Production Rate	(Btu/Year)
TGXT	Total Gas Excise Tax	(1975 $/Btu)
TIMN	Technology Investment Multiplier, Normal	(Dimensionless)
TOPR	Total Oil Production Rate	(Btu/Year)
TOXT	Total Oil Excise Tax	(1975 $/Btu)
WR	Wage Rate	(1975 $/Man-Year)
WRI	Wage Rate, Initial, 1950	(1975 $/Man-Year)
WRMP	Wage Rate Multiplier from Productivity	(Dimensionless)
WRMPT	Wage Rate Multiplier Table	

APPENDIX E

LIST OF EXOGENOUS VARIABLES IN ECONOMY1
THAT BELONG TO FOSSIL1

DCINV	Domestic Coal Investments	(1975 $/Year)
DCNCC	Domestic Coal Noncash Charges	(1975 $/Year)
DOINV	Domestic Oil Investments	(1975 $/Year)
DONCC	Domestic Oil Noncash Charges	(1975 $/Year)
IOCR	Imported Oil Consumption Rate	(Btu/Year)
IOTAR	Import Oil Tariffs	(1975 $/Btu)
NEAP	Net Energy Average Price	(1975 $/Btu)
NECR	Net Energy Consumption Rate	(Btu/Year)
NEEP	Net Energy Effective Price	(1975 $/Btu)
SEINV	Steam Electric Investments	(1975 $/Year)
SENCC	Steam Electric Noncash Charges	(1975 $/Year)
TGINV	Total Gas Investments	(1975 $/Year)
TGNCC	Total Gas Noncash Charges	(1975 $/Year)
TGPR	Total Gas Production Rate	(Btu/Year)
TGXT	Total Gas Excise Tax	(1975 $/Btu)
TOPR	Total Oil Production Rate	(Btu/Year)
TOXT	Total Oil Excise Tax	(1975 $/Btu)

INDEX

accelerated conservation policies, 146-49; effects on
distribution of income, 175;
effects on economic growth,
159; in ECONOMY1, 98,
109; in a labor-intensive
economy, 179; and subsi-
dies to capital and labor,
86

actions (social, economic,
and political), 25

capital accumulation process,
43-45, 130-40

capital deepening process, 46,
176

capital to labor ratio, 177-79;
behavior of (in ECONOMY1),
177-79; in a labor-intensive
economy, 179

capital rental rate, 26, 101

causal structure, of ECON-
OMY1, 59; in system
dynamics method, 15

conflict among factors of production, 21-26; and inflation, 25-26; and produc-
tivity growth, 25-26

conservation policies, see,
accelerated conservation
policies

deflator mechanism in
ECONOMY1, 85-86

depletion of oil and gas, 2

depreciation allowances, 101

deregulation policies, 146;
effects on domestic energy
production, 158; effect on

economic growth, 158; effects
on equity, 167-75; of oil and
gas prices, 146

desired share of income, 22; in a
neo-classical world, 28; in a
world with satisficing firms,
29-30

disequilibrium effects, 14, 46-47

distributive shares (see also,
shares of income): conflict
over, 21-26; and factor substitution, 26-30

disturbances, 24-25

Duesenberry, James S., 20

dynamic behavior: modes of
ECONOMY1, 130-40; and neoclassical model, 14

DYNAMO: equations, 61

economic entities, 24-25

economic growth, 2-3; determinants of, 19; energy and,
149-59

elasticity of substitution, 8;
tests with alternate assumptions, 77-79

EMF Model, 9-10

energy demand: sector of
ECONOMY1, 103-10

energy/economy interactions, 2,
19; due to energy price, 130-
33; due to energy shortages,
130-33; and factor substitution,
29-30, 54; neo-classical theory
of, 7-9

energy policies (see also, deregulation policies and accelerated conservation policies):
145-49; excise tax, 146;
tariffs on imports, 146

215

ABOUT THE AUTHOR

NARASIMHAN KANNAN is an economist and an engineer working on advanced energy systems at the METREK division of MITRE Corporation.

ry